A GUIDE TO BALANCING **LIFE'S ACHIEVEMENTS**

Simple Living IN A COMPLEX WORLD

SECOND EDITION

DAVID IRVINE

WILEY

John Wiley & Sons Canada Ltd.

MAY 27 2004

National Library of Canada Cataloguing in Publication

National Library of Canada Cataloguing in Publication

Irvine, David, 1956-

  Simple living in a complex world : a guide to balancing life's achievements / David Irvine.

ISBN 0-470-83464-1

1. Self-realization. I. Title.
BF637.S4I79 2004   158.1   C2004-901552-4

Production Credits:

Cover design: Sharon Foster
Text design: Adrian So R.G.D.
Cover photo photographer/artist: Sandra Baker - Getty Images
Printer: Tri-Graphic Printing Ltd.

Printed in Canada
10 9 8 7 6 5 4 3 2 1

Dedication

*To my parents, Joyce and Harlie, who taught
me the difference between knowledge and
wisdom, between a successful life and a
meaningful life, and the importance
of opening your compassionate heart.*

Contents

Acknowledgments

The universe is made of stories, not atoms.

— Muriel Rukeyser

Hundreds of people have had an impact on me in the development of this book. My sincere thanks to:

All of my workshop participants and clients who have taught me so much over the years, and specifically those who have given me permission to tell their stories in this book. Fictitious names have been used to protect their anonymity.

Don Loney at Wiley, for believing in this project and for his passionate vision. This is a better book because of Don's trust, his passion for this work, and his thoughtful perspective along the way.

Wendy Ross, who put her whole heart and soul into the original manuscript. She was able to take hundreds of pages of ramblings and musings, capture my voice, and turn it into a book.

Acknowledgments

My friends and colleagues, Bruce Klatt, Murray Hiebert, Bernie Novokowsky, Shaun Murphy, and George Campbell, for their years of support and encouragement to bring more of myself to my work, both in my writing as well as in my consulting and speaking.

All of the Holistic Resource Management practitioners, who have taught me the difference between a quality of life and a standard of living.

Peter Johnston, Blake Holtman, Walter Brust, Don Campbell, and Susan Levin, whose friendships have greatly influenced my life and work.

Ross Gilchrist, for his ability to help me discover, clarify, and believe in my uniqueness.

My original editor at Redstone, Janet Alford, who added a new dimension to enhance the book's universal appeal. Her reassuring voice on the telephone helped me to stay on course. She brought it all together.

Tony King, Patti Kerfoot, Joan Anderton, Jerry Weinberg, Judy McCallum, Tyson Brust, Jim Soldan, and Grant Molyneux for their inspired and invaluable critique of the early manuscript.

The authors and teachers whom I have quoted throughout the book and who have inspired me.

My wife and life-long companion, Val, who came to me as a gift, who has believed in me for so many years, and has been beside me in all of my dreams. Her gift of presence, her patience, her compassionate heart, along with her editing skills made this all possible.

My three daughters, Mellissa, Hayley, and Chandra, for being such powerful teachers in my life and reminding me of what matters most.

My Creator, the source of all that is within these pages.

Preface

Over the years, numerous requests from friends, colleagues, and workshop participants to write a book led me to pen *Simple Living in a Complex World*. Their outer call was answered by an inner call to organize my observations onto the written page, and to share something of what I had learned. That first edition, published in 1997, struck an important chord within people across North America. Over the past seven years I have received hundreds of emails and letters, both from individuals personally and from those within companies, who have found a place for *Simple Living* in their homes and workplaces. During this time, many have attended my Simple Living Seminars™. Large numbers have expressed their gratitude for the value of this work and the contribution it has made to their lives. Many have shared their experiences with the "Reflect" and "Act" portions of the book, and told me their stories.

All of the feedback—whether thoughtful reflections, suggestions, insights, or the sharing of personal stories—has been enormously valuable in furthering my understanding of living a balanced life, and has advanced my own journey of finding simplicity in the complexity of our post-modern era. Indeed, I am shaped and enriched by these conversations and connections as we continue to create together an enhanced awareness and commitment to living a simpler life.

My desire in this revision is to pass along my new understanding of simple living that has been integrated into my life, my relationships, and work over the past seven years. The fruits of many of those early seeds planted in the words of that first edition back in 1997 are now ripening. Thus, I am compelled and called to pass along my new awareness of living simply.

I offer a simple introduction to personal change, one that has helped many people—including myself—rediscover the joys of living in today's complex world. As in the first edition, it is not my intention to offer a "how-to" self-help book, so much as to offer my thoughts on the journey towards self-discovery. I use real life stories and practical exercises to illustrate the road map of options available for those seeking peace in the midst of their busy lives.

We all live lives that are sometimes driven by necessity. Whether a corporate executive attempting to meet the expectations of shareholders and customers, a parent trying to do what is right for her children, an entrepreneur building a business, an employee in a large organization who is experiencing a hollow feeling from having sold out to the demands of others, or an exhausted helping professional whose load is getting heavy, any of us can become so busy putting out the fires around us that we lack time to kindle the fires of our own inner life. All too often we react to the stresses of daily life, rather than respond to our deeper desires. We begin to see, when we stop and pay attention to these deeper yearnings, that we are no longer living our own lives, but rather, in our harried and frantic world, our lives are living us. Life becomes a little too much like being on a boat where the oarsmen are all pulling with great enthusiasm in different directions, and in the frenzy, we stop listening to ourselves, to a deeper voice from within that is calling us to live life differently.

I believe that life can be different. In the first edition I suggested that the key to living simply is the ability to connect with ourselves and with others, and then to integrate those connections with our achievements in the world. The integration of connection and achievement, and the sense of fulfillment that grows from that integration, was the consistent message throughout that first book. In this revision, I add a third capacity on the path of simplicity. Although integrating achievements and connections remains vital to the journey, those who live simply in today's complex world have also discovered *contentment*.

Contentment lies below the surface of our achievements or our failures, our connections or our losses. Contentment does not mean to be in a place where there is no noise, trouble, or hard work. It means to be in the midst of those things and still be calm within. Contentment is not the same as the allure and fleeting emotion of happiness. Contentment is a lasting inner center that gives you freedom and serenity even in unhappiness. I have, in this revised edition, explored the area of contentment in great detail and have included a section with insights and clues for centering ourselves.

I use real life stories to illustrate my thinking, and I offer a series of "Reflect" and "Act" exercises at the end of each chapter. These exercises are intended to develop the reflective thought process necessary for contentment, and then to encourage you to follow through by taking action. The exercises are designed to foster harmony between the inner truth and the outer call to action that our busy lives demand.

I share the stories, experiences, and exercises in this book to inspire you and guide you to listen more intentionally and courageously to that deeper part of yourself, to uncover that place in your soul where hidden possibilities reside, a place of simple living.

one
CONSIDERING CHANGE

No problem can be solved from the same level of consciousness that it was created. We must learn to see the world anew.

—Einstein

Life's Vital Continuum— Living a Centered Life

*There is no greater sin than enslavement
to desire, no greater curse than discontent,
no greater misfortune than selfish craving.
Therefore, in being content, one will always
have enough.*

—Lao-Tsu, *Tao Te Ching*

It is no easy task to discover simplicity in today's complex world. In my workshops I ask people to simply stop and think about their lives. When they do, most are deeply concerned about the way we live. People express the level of strain they feel in all areas of their lives, about the increase in demands on them, about not having enough time for what matters most. Many express how, in our post-modern society, there is more information but less communication, more email and less connection, more conveniences but less time. Substantial contact with friends, with nature, and with ourselves where we can have solitude, silence, and time to attend to the voice within has all but vanished. Reflective time—the space needed for innovation and creativity—has disappeared from many of our work environments.

We dash here and there desperately trying to fulfill the many obligations that press upon us. We rush back and forth between business commitments, family responsibilities, and personal obligations. While we are busy responding to the needs of a parent, a child or a life-partner, we fear that our work will deteriorate. When we respond to the pressures of work, we fear we are failing in our personal relationships. On those occasional moments when we spend a few minutes with ourselves, we feel guilty that we are neglecting our community or social responsibilities. We are a culture, despite the abundance of resources surrounding us, where many feel restless, dissatisfied, and frustrated. Talk to any medical practitioner today and they will tell you of the significant increase in prescriptions to antidepressants and anti-anxiety medications in recent years. We are an intelligent society that has found a way into the vastness of outer space, we can view a DNA molecule, yet, in our fanaticism to accomplish great things and accumulate wealth, we are forgetting the art of living simply. Whether it be questions of overload, of frantic existence and harried survival, concerns of materialism and consumption, or anxiety about a loss of security, there is a pervasive skepticism that our fast-paced, consumptive society represents the highest form of human development. Intuitively, something just doesn't feel right, and even though it may be difficult to articulate, if we stop and listen we sense

3

that we are losing touch with something vital to our existence. Many find themselves asking that pervasive question, "Is this really the way we want to live?"

This *something* that is at odds within the world will not heal until we heal from *within*. The world will change when we change. Simple living begins with *inner* simplicity—the ability to live a centered life by finding a degree of peace, serenity, and sustained contentment, even in the midst of a complex world. Living a balanced life is not about divvying up each aspect of our life into equal portions, while frantically trying to balance all the pieces with equivalent attention. Balance doesn't mean hectically spending eight hours in a job, and then balancing it with madly meeting the demands of our loved ones and our community during the remaining waking eight hours, while attempting to squeeze in a few minutes for ourselves. Simple living is not merely a matter of downsizing, of living with less, or of working less. It is possible to do that with the result being nothing more than complex poverty.

A major premise of this book is that simplicity begins with an *internal* healing. Healing a fractured world begins with healing our internal world. I offer a story at this point to begin understanding the battle that often goes on inside of us. The story goes that there was an old yogi master who sat for years under a tree in the center of a busy city, meditating all day. At first, the business people and street vendors muttered among themselves, criticizing his lack of initiative.

Eventually, he became an accepted part of the scenery for most of the downtown core.

One day, a young businessman rushing to work, decided to stop and confront the old man. The businessman's anger had built daily as he watched the sleepy-looking yogi "lounging" in the park. "How is it you can sit here day after day in a trance?" he shouted.

"My son," replied the yogi, "perhaps you are the one who is in a trance."

This story illustrates two vital qualities to be discovered and balanced for simplicity to find herself in our lives. The businessman represents the achievements in our lives—the part in us that plans, pursues a dream, plants a flag and makes a mark in the world. The businessman is about strategy and exploration. He is about going out into the world and finding a place within it. The businessman is about focus, ambition, and tactics. He is about pioneering and adventuring into new territory.

Achievement is vital to progress and everyone has the ability to do great things and make their mark in the world. Building bridges, climbing mountains, and a thousand other things manifest personal achievement and satisfaction. We all measure ourselves against the demands of the world and by rising to the challenge we, and the world, are better for it.

The yogi master, conversely, represents a quality that is seldom spoken of in our modern world. The yogi demonstrates that rare trait, so vital to simplicity, called *gracefulness*[1]. Graceful living speaks to a kind of

5

---

[1] I gratefully acknowledge the work of Jerome Segal, in his book, *Graceful Simplicity: Toward a Philosophy and Politics of Simple Living,* for his contribution to my thinking about gracefulness as it relates to simplicity.

elegance in our approach to life. Gracefulness is about living fully, giving our life the time it deserves, whether it be with a child, with a loved one, our garden, or a sunset. Graceful living is one of those elusive expressions of life that is difficult to articulate, but, like beauty, you know when it is present, and you know when it is not. Gracefulness is a way of being in the world, a quality which is often debased by the rush of life, by ongoing "to-do" lists, and living like someone frantically racing through a mall with a shopping list, impatiently waiting for people to get out of our way. Grace holds the fire of connection—to our loved ones, to our community, and to a deeper, hidden self beyond what we often bring to our achievement-focused world. As we connect more fully with life, we attune to those we care about.

A sense of loneliness can be covered up by the things we do as we seek recognition and success. The shell of achievement both protects and isolates us. As we slow down, we break open this shell and find the seeds of grace within. Reveling in the energy of youth and discovering the wisdom of our elders, graceful living brings a sense of curiosity and wonder to whatever we do. Grace opens us to a renewed understanding of the world around us, and to the beauty and depth of each and every human being that, in our busyness, we so often miss. In our pursuit of more—more income, abundance, and achievement, we can end up divorcing ourselves from our truest self, and in the process, divorce ourselves from those that matter most to us.

To live more simply, we are called to be positioned in the world and to be graceful—to both achieve and connect—in our own unique way. Some would argue that grace alone will make our lives simpler. This may be true, especially in a culture like ours so in need of balance, but if you solely follow the way of graceful living, be prepared to live in poverty. Though this may be the course for some, a life without achievement is not my path.

On the other hand, a life of achievement without grace is an existence that also is out of balance; it lacks sustainability. Slowing down and finding a human pace, a tempo more connected to nature, brings out the value in our lives. We begin opening our compassionate hearts to our own lives and to those around us, and awaken to the need for meaning and creative expression of our unique gifts in the service of others. When we give life the attention it deserves—by taking time to relax, to meditate, to just sit each day in silence to think or not to think, to listen to the voice from within, to just be—our lives can be transformed and simple living becomes our reward. When we act in haste, whether it be at work or with friends, our activity and ultimately our very being become a mere means to some intended outcome; we miss out on the experience of living at all. In *Walden*, Henry David Thoreau looked about the world and saw it as mostly "foolishness— people not knowing how to grab hold of the gift of life."[2] When our frantic way of being in the world becomes our familiar way, we have failed in what

2 Ibid, p. 16

Thoreau identified as the great enterprise—to make living poetic.[3]

Responding to the demands of *society*—from our loved ones, our boss, or the community—is necessary for us to feel a part of the world and fulfilled in the world. Yet continually reacting to the needs of others can drown out the desires of the *soul*—time to relax, to notice a sunset, to just *be* with ourselves or with people we care about—and distance us from the desires of our soul. Both are needed if we want a simple life. By neglecting either society's demands or our soul's desire, we create a fracture inside of us, a misalignment between the choices we are making and our core values. We must both be in the world *and* be responsive to the needs of the soul, in order to sustain simplicity. Simplicity, in this light, comes from within. It is a way of being in the world, in the midst of the outside noise, demands, and work. Simplicity is not necessarily about working less, but it is about the way we bring ourselves to our work.

In order to achieve simplicity in our lives by integrating our achievements with our deepest connections, we must find our balance. Coming to balance is easier when you have a strong inner foundation upon which to place the fulcrum. Integrating achievement with grace upon a lasting center promises a result of contentment along with the simplicity.

Alignment, or living a centered life, begins with an internal North Star, an interior frame of reference that becomes the center or driving force of a person's life

8

[3] Ibid., p. xvi.

around which everything revolves. It is the anchor, the foundation of all activities, relationships, and decisions. As we find that unifying center within, we no longer get our security and worth from our achievements, our relationships, our roles, or our possessions. So much of our lack of simplicity today is not so much about the complexity of the world as it is about a lack of a firm center within us upon which to stand.

The center of your life is that which gives you security, worth, identity, and sustenance. Many find their center in their *work*, and work defines them rather than fulfils them. For others, their center lies in their *achievements*, in the *prestige* and *recognition* they receive from the world. Still others find their center in themselves, and become *self*-centered. We have all met people who are centered on their *children*, where instead of an opportunity for the expression of love, their children become the defining force in their lives. Many center themselves on an addiction and *escape reality* to center themselves. Still others are attached to their possessions for their worth. For many years, when I practiced as a therapist, my center was aligned with being *needed* in the world and with being *approved* of by others.

It is human to attach ourselves to these various external barometers for our merit and our confidence. When we are first starting a career, we may well find ourselves centering our life on our career as a way of positioning ourselves in the world. If you have ever attended university or an intensive education program, you know about the expectation of centering your life on the learning experience. For those who have spent time in a significant relationship, especially if you entered it at a young or vulnerable time in your life, you will know the experience of being centered on a relationship, particularly in the initial stages. In the early years of child rearing, it is natural—and probably vital—to attach ourselves to our children. If you have experienced success or the recognition that comes from achievement in your life, you know how seductive it can be to become overly identified with acknowledgment from the world. For helpers, it is common to over-identify with those we serve. If you have ever started a business, you know that your life will be centered around your business for a time while you help it take root.

"Everybody has a hungry heart," wrote Bruce Springsteen. What does your heart hunger for? What defines you? What gives you worth? What is your source of sustaining strength? What gives you security? Although there are times when these external attachments are appropriate and even necessary to our source of worth, the key is to not allow these attachments to define us for extended periods of our life. By centering ourselves on external standards, we will never feel completely satisfied.

If we are centered on materialism to define us, we will plunge ourselves into debt and then take two or three jobs to stay afloat. We uproot our families with unnecessary moves just so we can have a more prestigious house. If we are centered on our children, we will discover the pressure we unknowingly put on them to carry our self-worth, experience the excruciating pain of letting go, or find them living with us long after our parental shelf life is up. We are aware of the emptiness, the loneliness that emerges from chronic self-centered-ness, or the destructive and despairing path left by a person whose life is centered around an addictive sub-stance. For the addict, one hit will never satisfy, and a thousand hits are never enough. If we are centered on our work or achievements to give us worth, the workday will never end. Work, for many, has turned into an addiction where there is never enough time to fill the unquenchable thirst for more—more achievement, more success, more recognition, and more money. How often do we stop and ask, "How much is enough?" or "What is the quality of life I am trying to create?"

With a center in the external, comes the inevitabil-ity of impermanence. All external means of self-identity are, of course, temporary. The children will leave home. We will one day be unemployed. Our life-part-ner will not always be there. Aging affects health. Wealth is tenuous. And finally, no one will ever get out of this world alive.

Simplicity slips from our grasp when we are centered on the fleeting allure of achievement, approval from oth-ers, possessions, or prestige. Simplicity obviously calls us to find a balance and moderation in all our various attachments, and to integrate the achievements of our life

11

with the vital connections. But to find simplicity we must also find a sustaining center from which a deep sense of contentment emerges, independent of our roles, our achievements, our connections, and our possessions.

From acknowledging this fracture, or misalignment, and in listening to the stories and experiences of hundreds of people over these past seven years, a third piece of the simplicity puzzle has emerged, a piece that is independent of our connections and our achievements. While teaching the achieve/connect continuum, I met people who could not relate to achievement and connection as a continuum at all. For many, their greatest "achievements" were in their connections, and their greatest "connections" were actually in their achievements. And even though I was leading people to integrate achievement into connections, a polarity remained between the two ends of the continuum. Simple living could only find its home in an undertaking that lay beyond achievement and connection.

Inner simplicity—or contentment—is what I have come to call the third and most vital key to simple living. Contentment does not mean being in a place where there is no noise, trouble, or hard work. It means being in the midst of those things and remaining calm within. You are calm not just because you have a balance between your achievements and your connections, but because your achievements or connections no longer define you. You are centered from within and fulfilled by your various roles,

achievements, relationships, but you are no longer owned by these. Your worth comes from a deeper source that lies beyond what the world offers.

The centered life, that place of contentment, lies deep below the surface of our external environment and is independent of achievements and failures, connections and losses, wealth or poverty, work or rest, doing or being. Common to all on the path of simplicity, the centered life is about finding that deep inner foundation upon which to stand that gives you the clarity to say "No," as well as "Yes," with certainty and conviction. The centered life gives you a solid inner rudder in the currents of your external circumstances. While your career, net worth, possessions, and relationships may define your social status, simplicity is defined by your inner condition. Contentment, and the promise of both simplicity and freedom from the demands of the world, will emerge as we begin to let go of the need for approval. After all, be careful about keeping up with the Joneses. As soon as you catch up with them, they are sure to refinance!

Simplicity involves an inner condition. It means clarity of purpose and honesty within. We begin to avoid the exterior clutter of many possessions irrelevant to our sense of purpose. We can enjoy our possessions, but they no longer define us. We can be fulfilled in our work, for it no longer identifies us. We are no longer owned by others; nor are we slaves to the tyranny of approval and prestige. Simplicity—standing on a solid

13

inner center—means an ordering and guiding of our energy and our desires, a prudent restraint in many directions in order to secure a greater abundance of a few directions. It is like returning to our own familiar home, our familiar routines, and our comfortable old bed after a long trip. Living a centered life is like traveling far away, responding to the pull of the world, and then coming home to yourself.

A lack of freedom, which deprives us of any resemblance of simplicity, means being governed by compulsions. Real simplicity means to be free to know who we are, with all that is beautiful, and all the brokenness in us; it is to love our own values, to embrace them, and to develop them; it is to be anchored in a vision and a truth but also to be open to others and, so, to change. Freedom lies in discovering that truth is not a set of fixed certitudes but a mystery we enter into, one step at a time. It is a process of knowing there is an oasis, but also being patient with ourselves; we won't always hit the mark. As humans, we circle around it, but knowing where our lasting security and subsequent serenity is *not*—in our roles, our achievements, our relationships—is our first step toward the oasis.

Aristotle believed that there were some people who were "natural slaves," in that they lacked the capacity of governing themselves.[4] By depending on a life outside of ourselves for our worth, we become slaves to the tyranny of demands of others, to the needs and approval of others. When we need prestige in the world for a sense

14

4 Ibid., p. 9.

of our own worth, we become slaves to our desires for more. Think of what you do when you spend beyond your means and enter the world of debt. You give another power over your liberty. Human identity is no longer defined by who we are, but by what we own. There is emptiness in the existence of consumption. We have discovered that simply owning things and consuming them does not satisfy our longing for meaning. With the appetite of consumption, simple living itself gets consumed. With frugality comes freedom. Attuning to life with grace, whether in a beautiful city or the unspoiled countryside, has the power to liberate us from the impermanence of consumption. The point of an economy, even a dynamic economy, is not to have more and more; it is to liberate us from the economic—to provide a platform from which we may go forth to build the good life. That is, according to Jerome Segal, the *Alternative American Dream*.[5]

What will free us from the tyranny of the demands placed upon us? The answer is in a unifying center that is independent of our achievements and our failures, our connections and our losses. Finding a sustaining center lies at the heart of simplicity. It means honesty from within, clarity of our core values, and courage to align our life's choices with what matters most. Simplicity is standing on a foundation of principles rather than on popularity, on courage rather than comfort, on deep self-respect rather than the fleeting allure of materialism or prestige.

[5] Ibid., p. 12.

15

My journey to discover a lasting center from which to live began abruptly on the early morning of March 17, 1993, when I was beckoned to a centered life through the pain of missing my daughter's birth. For the past four years I had been traveling in excess of a hundred and fifty days a year. The irony is that my life was out of balance in my attempts to teach others how to achieve more simplicity in their lives. Hayley was born early, and despite what I thought were adequate precautions, I was simply too busy working—achieving—to be realistic and make it to Val's side in time. Never have I felt so desperate, so powerless, and so regretful, as I was that night when I took that call from the hospital while pacing alone in a hotel room. I had originally anticipated getting home two days later, but children are born on a timetable much bigger than my strategic plan and willful intentions. Some things in life simply cannot be run like a business—with strategy, goals, and structure. It was the obstetric nurse that night who explained to me that Val had desperately tried to reach me, during her initial contractions, on my pager and at the hotel where I was staying, but both connections had somehow broken down. It was then that Val, in my neglectful absence, had to call a friend and was rushed to the hospital. By the time the nurse was finally able to reach me, Val was in the final stages of labor and was due to give birth within two hours.

I frantically tried to charter a helicopter that morning, but learned that I would not make it to Val's side to

16

be with her, and I missed Hayley's birth. Exhausted and despairing at both my failures and my disconnections, I sat back in my chair. Indeed, in my drive to achieve, I had failed at grace. I had several hours before the next flight would actually arrive home, to reflect on how out of balance my life was, and how far away it was from the simplicity that I was teaching others to attain. When I would overwork, driven by the demands of my clients, I would feel guilty about neglecting those that I loved. When I spent time connecting, I would feel guilty about not living up to my expectations—both from myself and others—for my desired achievements. Thus, I was always preoccupied and never fully present in life. As I awaited the flight to take me to my life-partner, our newborn child, and a new commitment to a simpler life, a deep realization of how fractured my life had become surfaced on that cold spring morning. Finding a lasting center has come to me through the pain of an emotional break*down* and subsequent break*through*. Although I do not yet fully live a centered life with the clarity to do the right things and then taking the time to do them right, I know it is possible. A long road ahead awaits me. I am, at times, frightened, but I hope that I, and others like me who are embarking on this journey, know that we are not alone. On my quest for finding a center within, many days I still hold tightly to what people think of me. "If the admiration and love from others and my achievements were not there, if all that fell away, who would I be?" I often ask myself.

I know, however, that I must continue on the path, knowing that rejection, loneliness, pain, as well as joy, beauty, and wonder are all part of the journey. As I experience this entire spectrum from a sustained center, moments of contentment—and subsequently simplicity—emerge.

The antidote to the exhaustion that so many of us experience in this post-modern world is not rest but centeredness that comes from alignment. When our lives begin to be in line with our core values, with what matters most to us, and we integrate grace into our achievements, then we begin to step into a simpler life. My hope is that by opening the pages of this book you will open more fully this door within and begin the path of sustained simplicity.

Reflect:

Pick up some paper and your pen and consider the following:

1) Stop momentarily to reflect on the quality of your life. What is the degree of serenity in your life? Of inner peace?

2) Draw a horizontal line across the page. Label one end "connect" and the other end "achieve." Consider the three people who know you best. Where would they place you on your achieve/connect continuum? Write their names in the appropriate spots. Now where would you place yourself?

3) Make a list of three things you long to do and never have enough time for. If you did these things, which direction would you be moving on the continuum?

4) Consider your journey over time along this continuum. Where were you three years ago? If you are going to find the fulfillment you seek, where do you need to be three years from now?

5) Now, consider, "Where is your center? That is, where is the source of your worth? Where does your security come from? What sustains you?"

19

6) Consider those special elders you may know who live with grace and can reflect on their lives with gratitude in their accomplishments, peace in their relationships, and contentment within themselves. Let them set the standard to which you aspire.

7) Are you in need of some mentoring in this area of living a centered life? Of finding contentment and grace from within?

Opening to Possibilities

The universe is made of stories, not atoms.

—Muriel Rukeyser

Centuries before the beginning of formal religions, storytelling was the means for passing on the ancient wisdom. Within the stories, deep truths about life found their expression. Stories introduced listeners to the world of enchantment and mystery and have long been the traditional tool of teaching and learning. All great teachers throughout time have captured their wisdom in stories around campfires and in tribal gatherings, on hillsides and in sanctuaries, drawing listeners to profound visions of life with images and symbols.

Many of us need to read or hear a good story, in order to awaken us to our own story. Each person's story is about all of us. This book is a collection of teaching stories, both from my own experience, from the experiences of those I have met and worked with, and from some of the great traditions. Anecdotes and tales of personal experience carry the power to illuminate truth, heal fractured lives, and inspire change. Storytelling engages the imagination, drawing us away from the complexity of life to a place where the world feels simpler and all of our deepest longings seem possible. The act of sharing a good story can open a path to a new insight that has been closed off by the demands of adult life. Storytelling can change lives.

I recall such a life-changing story in my youth, when, at the age of ten, my parents read Wilson Rawl's modern classic, *Where the Red Fern Grows* to me. I remember being a shy, insecure, reserved, and isolated fourth-grader, somewhat disconnected from my own nature. Sitting on my father's lap, I recall vividly Rawl's story of ten-year-old Billy Coleman growing up in the Ozark Mountains of North Eastern Oklahoma. Billy's struggles, sacrifices, joys, and tragedies as he pursues his dream to own, train, and compete with his own coonhounds captured my imagination.

As Billy's days of innocent boyhood come to a close, he is left with wonderful memories and a beautiful legend, which gives sacred meaning to those memories. What remains for me, over thirty-five years later, is the vivid memory of sitting in my father's arms enthralled by the picture painted through Rawl's captivating words. Billy Coleman's journey became my journey. Billy Coleman's adventure became my adventure. Those dark hills of the Ozark Mountains became my own gloomy forest. Billy Coleman's call to adventure and resulting grief and growth became my call to adventure and subsequent growth into a fiercer, more courageous, more confident adolescent. Reading about Billy's courage to stand up to a mountain lion enabled me to face bullying in the school playground by walking away and maintaining my self respect.

Perhaps the most affecting story that my father told me, however, came not from the pages of a book, but from his own experience. It was years later, when my aging father took me for a walk in the inner streets of modern Calgary. We sat down on a park bench and he told his story as a youth worker on these same streets in the 1930s and 1940s. The old South YMCA where he worked was now replaced with office buildings. He reminisced for several minutes, reflecting on the unlived life. With emotions welling up, he told me of how he had abandoned his calling in life to work with youth, and surrendered to society's demand to get a better paying, more prestigious position. He expressed how he developed a hollow feeling from selling out to the pressures of the world instead of listening to his heart and following the voice of a deeper current within.

"My life was far more complicated than it needed to be, not because of my workload, but because my work was misaligned with my calling—my deepest values—in my life. I spent my life as an administrator, but I was meant to stay right here, to work with these kids."

There was an extended pause as he gathered his composure.

"David, don't ever give up on living the life you are meant to live. Listen carefully to your inner voice, to the wisdom that comes when you step away from the noise of the world."

There was another pause.

"David, may you find and honor your gifts, and may you find a way to serve the world through these gifts."

Although I had little comprehension of the depth of wisdom that was afforded to me that fall afternoon, the memory that remains is both the anguish of regret and the contentment of gratitude.

Soon after this conversation, my father decided, at the age of sixty-five, to muster the courage of his own advice. Telling his story of a career that stifled many of his gifts was as helpful to him as it was to me. Deeming that it was never too late to change the course of his life, he returned to university to further his education, not in social planning or administration, but in art, a submerged passion he sustained all his life. Three years later he was taken far too early from this earth by a brain aneurism, but his life, along with his stories and his wisdom, remain and continue to grow within me. Dad's cautionary tale has become a filter for my career choices, and I carefully assess each opportunity for alignment with my core values and gifts.

A recent conversation gave me another opportunity to see how storytelling often helps the teller as much as the listener. I had concluded a session with a group of senior executives at a retreat center. After all the participants had left, I began packing up my materials preparing for the long drive home. Suddenly I looked up and one of the hotel housekeepers was standing by the side table leafing through some of my books.

"You like storytelling, don't you," she said.

"Why yes," I replied. "How would you know?"

"I was not just cleaning today," she responded. "I was also listening."

An intriguing silence fell on the conversation.

"Seeing as you like to hear stories, would you like to hear one?" she asked.

Tired, and ready to get home, I wasn't really in the mood for any more conversations, but something inside said, "Stop and listen. This woman has something to teach you."

So I sat and politely nodded, motioning for to her to continue.

"I came to this country ten years ago from Pakistan. I brought little with me except my children and one set of clothes. I worked hard to support my children as a single parent [she had apparently been abandoned at some point by her husband]. I grew very depressed, and wanted to take my own life, as the loneliness of living in a new culture with little support was growing to be unbearable. At a bus stop, I found the number for the distress line, and I called out as a plea for help.

"The woman on the suicide help line began the conversation by asking me to talk about my depression, and what might be causing me to be depressed.

"I don't want to talk about my depression," I replied. "Tell me a story. I just want to listen to a story."

"About what?" the woman asked.

"Anything. Just tell me a story. Tell me about your day. Your life. Your dreams."

"The volunteer fumbled through an anecdote, something that had happened to her earlier that day, dealing with one of her children."

"Thank you," replied the woman. "I will call you again." And she hung up.

A few days later, this woman called the suicide line again and, when a volunteer answered, she again said, "Tell me a story."

"Oh, you're the woman who we've been waiting for. Please hold on a minute. There's a person here who wants to talk with you."

She then went and got the volunteer who had been there on her first call. This time she was prepared with a story.

Tears filled the eyes of this woman as her recounting of the volunteer's story unfolded. Each day, this woman would call and request a story, and each day, the volunteer would share a new story about finding significance and perspective in the tasks and predicaments of daily life..

"Listening to these stories healed me," she said.

"Telling them was also undoubtedly healing for the helpers on the other line," I replied.

Reflect:

The aim of this chapter is to begin to have you think about stories, and the vital importance of stories as a tool to help you to listen more attentively to yourself as you begin taking steps toward a simpler, more balanced life. Pick up some paper and your favorite pen and consider the following...

1) Reflect on the storytellers in your life. Who has told you stories that have impacted you?

2) What powerful stories are still vivid in your mind that might have been told to you, even in childhood? Consider a parent, a relative, or a mentor whose stories remain as bright and evocative today as they did when you first heard them.

3) What story from your own life stands out as one that connects with you, that inspires you to reflect on living life more simply? How might you use this awareness of story in your life to align your life more with what matters most?

4) What is your story? What satisfies you? What do you yearn for?

A Wake-up Call

There are two things to aim at in life: first to get what you want, and after that to enjoy it. Only the wisest of mankind achieve the second.

—L.P. Smith

The search for a simpler life might begin when we notice an uncomfortable sense of incongruity between our outer achievement and our inner desires. Somehow, the pieces of our lives may not fit together well. The picture we live in feels more like a muddled collage than that beautifully expressed work of art we aspire to. For many of us, however, the incongruity may be present but we just haven't recognized it. Still others will sense the discomfort, but feel much too busy to launch a search for harmony and balance at the moment.

In spite of the fact that we feel too busy to change, the reality may be that our current pace and path cannot be maintained indefinitely. Sometimes, we drive ourselves directly into a brick wall. The brick wall of personal crisis may be about to stop us in our tracks (or maybe it already has). I think of such crisis as a wake-up call, a loud and clear signal that something needs to change.

A great example of the wake-up call in action is Bob's story. Bob was a successful executive but he was heading directly into his own brick wall...

I met Bob at a conference where I gave a presentation on managing personal and organizational transition. I knew every person at the conference was financially successful. No one in the room was earning less than a six-figure income. At the end of my presentation, I expressed the wish that each of the executives would find, in his or her own way, a life of meaning beyond the accumulation of wealth or achievement.

After I finished, Bob approached me, obviously emotional. "Can you recommend a counselor?" he asked. "I'm in the middle of a crisis and I don't have anyone to talk to." Although I was no longer running a family therapy practice, I scheduled an appointment. I spent our first counseling session hearing Bob's story.

Bob was a geologist for a large oil company. He traveled throughout the Middle East. He was home fewer than sixty days a year. His lifestyle epitomized success. He had a luxurious home, a wife and children, full access to the company jet, and an income in excess of several hundred thousand dollars a year.

One day, Bob received notice from his employer that he was about to be laid off. A few days later, he received notice from a lawyer that his wife was about

29

to file for divorce. Bob flew home to plead the case for his marriage, but his wife would not see him. In despair, he climbed behind the wheel of his half-ton truck and drove it over an embankment into the river. The truck rolled three times. Bob walked away from the accident unscathed.

Bob found himself on the riverbank weeping over his inability to even kill himself. He looked down at the battered heap of metal lying in the river and saw the shattered remains of his life. Somehow, in that moment, he chose to begin a new search, a search to understand the meaning in his life rather than to end it. Shortly afterwards, we met at the conference.

When Bob finished telling his story he sat for a moment, then looked at me and said, "You know, I've always felt that success was something outside of me." I asked if he had ever talked with anyone like this before. "No," he replied. "Congratulations," I said. "Perhaps this crisis is the best thing that has ever happened to you."

Although I know he didn't understand my meaning, he felt good about looking at anther definition for success. The next month, he returned to my office with his wife. For three hours they sat with their knees and hearts touching, crying in each other's arms. His wife told him she didn't want a divorce, but she also wasn't prepared to go on living the way they had been. At the end of the session, after they had been honest with one another in a way that hadn't happened in seventeen years of marriage, Bob's wife turned to her husband and said, "This crisis is probably the best thing that has ever happened to you." He still didn't understand.

Bob continued to see me for two years. He needed time to slow down, face the chaos of change, and establish connections with himself and those closest to him. Eventually, and after much soul-searching, he and his family moved to another part of the country, where he chose to start a landscaping business built on his lifelong desire to work with his hands in the soil.

When I visited Bob and his family a few years later, his marriage was thriving and the teenage sons worked in the family business. The family had moved from a 4,500-square-foot mansion to a 1,100-square-foot bungalow. As he showed me his rock garden, he talked with pride about his love for the land and his new-found connection to himself, his family and his work. Bob smiled as he asked me if I had any idea how much money he made. He had traveled from an income of several hundred thousand a year to net earnings of just under $17,000. "You know, I've never been poorer in my life, and I've never been happier," he confided.

A few years later, I had the good fortune to speak with Bob again. With time and persistence, he was now running an extremely successful, and personally rewarding, entrepreneurial business. This time financial success did not change him. He was still living a simple, meaningful life.

"You really can have it all," he told me, "your dream job, your dream family, and all the financial resources you need. And do you know what?" he concluded. "I have to admit, that crisis was the best thing that ever happened to me."

Bob's wake-up calls were harsh. He hit an emotional rock bottom and survived a near-death experience. Somewhere he found the courage to ask for help; then he found the courage to change. He began to redefine his life so that both connection and achievement grew in harmony. Ultimately, he found a quality of life he never knew was possible.

Bob's story teaches us that a wake-up call can take the form of a threat to our financial security. One of the challenges in this process, then, may be to follow Bob's example and loosen our attachment to our possessions. It's easy to lose sight of the fact that material goods can shift as easily as sand castles. We all know that it's great to have money and the things that money can buy, and the options that money will give you. We can also spot the truth in the old adage, "Money doesn't buy happiness, but it pays for the illusion that it does." Yet many of us adopt an achievement ethic that eventually erodes our perspective about what is important. We build a business at the expense of our personal relationships; we make a living at the expense of a life; we get fit at the expense of our health; we drive ourselves to the point of obsessive ambition at the expense of our souls.

Wake-up calls are opportunities to examine the pace and path of our lives. When we devote as much energy to cultivating lasting relationships as we devote to growing our outer achievements, then we will have taken a great step towards quality of life as well as standard of living. Our lives can become beautifully structured works of art. We just need to stop occasionally and ask ourselves, "What values am I committed to preserve?"

I hope one of the values we will preserve is a commitment to a vital life. Harmony and vitality will not grow from achievement alone. They will emerge from sustained attention to connected relationships within our families, our communities, our business organizations, and ourselves. They will also emerge from finding the courage to seek achievement where our real passions lie. For me, Bob's journey is a story of success and contentment, in the most profound sense of those words.

Reflect:

Consider the most difficult challenge you have faced in the past three years (or maybe it is more appropriate for you to think about a challenge you are facing right now.) Jot down a few notes to awaken your memory. Reflect on the obstacles you faced, and the inner strength that resulted, as you lived through this challenging time. Was this a wake-up call? Can you identify how you changed as a result of this experience: what your life was like before, what happened, and what it is like now? Despite the difficulty, could it possibly be that this was the best thing that ever happened to you?

Wake-up calls carry important lessons. Can you list three lessons which this difficult experience may have taught you? Are you living now as though you learned those lessons?

Maybe I Am Fortunate

*It is not so much that we're afraid of change and
uncertainty, or so in love with the old ways, but it's
that place in between that we fear... It's like being
in between trapezes. It's Linus when his blanket is
in the dryer. There's nothing to hold on to.*

—Marilyn Ferguson

Whether you face a wake-up call of unnerving propor-
tions, or you have decided to simplify your life a bit, or
your regular route to work has just gone under construction, you have an opportunity to consider your
attitude towards change. Charlie Brown and his pals
haven't survived all these decades because they have
nothing to teach us about ourselves. We all know from
experience why Linus feels so lost without his blanket.
The familiar, even the tattered, worn-out familiar, holds
great comfort. That dizzying space in between trapezes is quite another matter.

We may go looking for change, or change may
come looking for us. Either way, change will happen. When it does, it will usually be accompanied by

35

temporary chaos. Our attitude towards change, and our response to its chaos, is crucial to both peace of mind and possibility for growth. The old story of the White Stallion teaches us one stance we might adopt in the face of change...

Once a King owned a magnificent white stallion. People traveled from far and wide to admire the steed and to praise the King. "Sir, you are most fortunate to own such a fine horse," they chorused.

After much consideration the King replied, "One cannot tell the fortune of another in such a short span of time. Maybe I am fortunate I own such a magnificent stallion. Maybe I am not. Only time will tell." The people left confused.

One day, the King went to his stables only to discover that the magnificent steed had jumped the fence and escaped. His subjects gathered around him and offered their condolences on his great loss. "It is so unfortunate that you have lost your fine steed, my Lord!"

The King replied, "One cannot tell the misfortune of another in such a short span of time. Maybe I am unfortunate to have lost my stallion. Then again, maybe I am fortunate. Only time will tell." Now the people were greatly confused.

Another day, to the bewilderment of all, the King's stallion returned. The stallion was followed by a beautiful mare. Then the people were a little less confused. All those who had offered their condolences on his loss flocked to the King and offered their congratulations on his new mare. "You are so fortunate to have this beautiful new mare, my Lord!"

Once again the King replied, "Maybe I am fortunate. Maybe I am not. Only time will tell." Once again the people left confused.

Some time after that, the King's only son was breaking the spirited mare. The Prince was thrown from the mount and broke his leg. The people rallied to offer their condolences yet again. "Your son is most unfortunate!" they cried.

The King's only reply was, "Maybe my son is unfortunate. Maybe he is not. Only time will tell."

Not long after, the army arrived to gather all the healthy young men to go to war. Many would never return. The Prince was spared, because his leg had not yet fully mended. At last, the people were no longer confused.

The story teaches us that our most devastating curses are often our greatest blessings, and our greatest blessings are often our most devastating curses. What we perceive as a blessing may in fact bring disaster, and what we perceive as disaster will ultimately hold some blessing. We can never fully predict the fortune or misfortune which change and chaos bring to our lives. Events that appear to be misfortunes may ultimately present hidden opportunities. Each of us must discover how to face the unknown world. We must determine what attitude we will bring to the space between trapezes.

In the late 1970s, my entire life was about training for the 1980 Summer Olympics. My entire being was committed to this preparation. My school, my marriage, everything was taking a back seat to my compulsion to make the national track and field team. Then events completely beyond my control knocked me right off my high-flying trapeze. I was devastated to learn that my country had declared a boycott of the Summer Olympic Games. I was angry and I was also lost.

It took some time, but eventually I began to notice how empty my life had been as a physical education major. I started to wonder about my narrow focus and direction. I began to consider my priorities. I had been so obsessed with running, I was unaware of anything else that was happening in my life. I was also mostly denying reality; in fact, making the Olympic team was a goal I was unlikely to achieve. That fall, I found myself in an early childhood education class and discovered a passion which was previously buried. Ultimately I changed university majors. Life has never been the same. That Olympic boycott was the best thing that could have happened to me.

We have all witnessed these disaster-turned-blessing, or blessing-turned-disaster experiences: a friend whose divorce turned out to be the best thing that ever happened; a colleague whose layoff, like Bob's, opened unseen possibilities; a neighbor whose young niece won the lottery and who two years later entered a drug rehabilitation center. Life is about change, and chaos, and integrating conflicting experiences into a meaningful whole...

The English essayist Charles Lamb tells the tale of an ancient village where raw pork was once considered to be a delicacy, perhaps not unlike sushi is today. One night there was a terrible house fire in the village. The family's best efforts were ineffective in extinguishing the blaze. Everything was lost.

The next day, the family was picking through the rubble and ashes, trying to find anything that could be salvaged. The youngest son found that the family pig had, unfortunately, perished in the fire. Exploring the beast's remains, the son discovered the delicious-ness of roast pork.

After that, there was a rash of house fires in the village.

All attempts at humor aside, the tough truth about change is that life usually gets harder before it gets better. I know that change is not easy, and I know that it takes more than a Pollyanna attitude to cope with chaos. Learning to make friends with change is a life-long challenge. I also know, however, that in order to thrive we will be required to change, and that change will move us toward growth if we can remain open to the possibilities. In our world, it's not the toughest that thrive, or even those most blessed with genius. It's those most capable of change.

39

In Enterprise, Alabama, there stands a monument honoring the South's worst agricultural pest, the boll weevil. The plaque on the monument reads, "In profound appreciation of the boll weevil, and what it has done as the herald of prosperity." The explanation for this paradoxical tribute is simple. The people of the area, their cotton fields devastated by boll weevils, were forced to turn to a new crop in order to survive. They converted their lands to raise peanuts. They have since experienced the greatest prosperity the region has ever known.

So the next time what appears to be a calamity strikes, and you get knocked off your trapeze, remember the boll weevils. Consider that every challenge has within it the seed of greater opportunity. Recognize disaster-turned-blessing-in-disguise as a part of life. As Tom Hanks once said, "You learn much more from getting your butt kicked than from getting it kissed." Or as my dad used to say (quoting Tom Watson, the founder of IBM), "If you want to be more successful, just double your failure rate!" If you can, welcome change with an open mind and a sense of humor. In the end, change is not only inevitable, it is also our only hope for the future.

Reflect:

Can you spot the boll weevil in your life, destroying all your cotton, attacking the familiar, driving you crazy, and in the process inviting you to plant peanuts? If you stopped trying to stamp out this unbeatable pest, and became willing to consider another option, what might you have an opportunity to accomplish instead?

Act:

For the next seven days, practice the King's response to change. Suspend all judgment of the chaos and tumult of life. Every time change happens, recite these lines (out loud is usually best, depending on who is within earshot):

Maybe I am unfortunate.
Then again maybe I am fortunate.
Only time will tell.

Write these lines on sticky notes and post them on your mirror, your desk, and the steering wheel of your car. Say them often. There is no doubt you will be presented with plenty of opportunity!

Rhythms

All life moves in rhythms. Molecules, tides, plants and animals, planets, human heartbeats, families, businesses, and each of our daily lives, everything moves in some form of rhythm. In my work, many of the people I meet struggle with the need to "manage time." Many of us live in one rhythm and at one speed: frantic and fast. The routine is becoming all too familiar. Each of us has our own version of hurry to work, run errands, rush to exercise, drive the kids to lessons, buy what we need, volunteer where we can. Most of us can sense, whether or not we like it, the pace we are setting for ourselves. However, we may be less able to sense how our pace is affected by, and is having an effect on, the people and the world around us.

One of the important principles of time and movement in the physical world is the concept of rhythmic entrainment.[1] *Entrainment* describes the process by which objects in motion synchronize with one another. Scientists have known for centuries that moving bodies tend to entrain. The most familiar example is the pendulum clock. If you place two out-of-sync pendulum clocks beside one another, they will eventually synchronize and will keep time together.

This operating principle of the physical world has something important to teach us about being human. Entrainment, you see, also applies to people. Like objects in space, we too "entrain," with one another, with our surroundings, and with the pace of our culture. Inevitably, and often outside our awareness, the rhythm of our lives is affected by the rhythm of those around us. We are also pulled to entrain with the rhythm of the modern world.

If we start to watch for this phenomenon, we will notice that we continuously entrain, however briefly, with other people. When someone smiles at me, I instinctively smile back. If someone comes into my office in an aggressive mood, I entrain with the hostility by becoming angry or defensive (or I expend a great deal of energy trying to stop that from happening). When I make a presentation, I am aware that my speech holds great power to capture or entrain the audience.

Even more important, though less often in our awareness, is our innate tendency to entrain with the

43

[1] I am indebted here to the work of Stephan Rechtschaffen, M.D., particularly his 1996 book *Time Shifting*, for introducing me to the concept of rhythmic entrainment. For details, see my Suggested Reading List at the back of this book.

rhythm of the modern world. I don't suppose it's controversial to suggest that the rhythm of the modern world is primarily built on the rhythms of technology. Technology brings us powerful tools and incredible capabilities. It also sets a brutal pace for us to follow. The rhythm of the modern world moves faster, and further from the rhythm of the natural world, with every technological innovation.

The pace of technology requires little description (and any attempt to do so is destined to become outdated almost immediately!). The instantaneous nature of communication, the velocity of travel, the processing rate of computers, the number of jolts per minute on television, all these speed up our perception of time and our reality. Few of us would choose to live in a world without the tools of communication, travel, information analysis, and entertainment which we use; certainly this would not be a popular suggestion in my business or in my household. However, rather than providing tools to simplify our lives, technology is running our lives as we continue to entrain to this vicious cycle. Living simply calls us to step back, to be mindful of what happens in us, and in our relationships, when we become overly entrained with the rhythms of technology.

For example, one of the rhythms of technology is fragmentation. Cellular phones, call-waiting signals, and paging devices are standard tools that many people, including me, use every day. As effective as these tools are, inevitably we allow their constant interruptions to enter our relationships and our inner lives. How many conversations did you try to have this week which were interrupted by your listener's (or your own, or a nearby diner's) cellular phone? How often have you felt the abrasiveness of just starting to open up with a person and they cut you off as they respond to the call waiting tone on their telephone? In laboratories, animals subjected to frequent, uncontrollable interruptions become nervous and eventually break down. In life, when we get too attached to our communication tools, we can find ourselves hovering on the edge of the next interruption rather than connecting with meaning in the present moment. Add television, a DVD player, and computer to the scenario and we might be losing the sanctuary of home to a hub of data reception and transmission.

Thirty years ago—just one generation—we had a party line on the farm, which meant that five households shared one phone line. If you wanted to make a phone call you often had to wait—sometimes up to one or two hours—until all your neighbors were off the line. Those were slower times, with more opportunity to entrain to nature's rhythm or at least to the rhythm of your neighbors. Think of where we have come since the 1970s. In the past thirty years we have moved from party lines to rotary phones to touch tone phones. Today we can feel frustrated, stressed, and tense because the voice activated calling function on our cell phone doesn't work within three seconds while we are speeding along

45

the highway at 120 km/hr! Is it any wonder that Bill Gates calls this the "age of velocity"?

Remember the days before emails and fax machines? It used to take up to two weeks to get a letter. In those days—less than two decades ago—we didn't expect a response for another week or two. Now, with instantaneous communication such as email, we have an expectation for—and often demand—a response to our email before our receiver has even had a chance to read it! Speaking of demands, ask any customer service representative in any organization today about the level of increase in demands from their customers and you will hear, "They want it done thoroughly, and they want it done yesterday!"

Even back in 1987, Jeremy Rifkin, in his ground-breaking and timely book, *Time Wars*[2], cited studies of people who accommodated themselves to the new sped-up time frame of the computer and became impatient with the slower durations of everyday clock culture. In clinical studies, psychologists observed that "computer compulsives" were much more intolerant of behavior that was "ambiguous, digressive, or tangential." In their interaction with spouses, family, and acquaintances, they were often terse, preferring simple yes-no responses. They were "impatient with open-minded conversations and uncomfortable with individuals who were reflective or meditative." "These so-called "computer compulsives" demand brevity and view social discourse in instrumental terms, interacting

[2] Jeremy Rifkin, *Time Wars: The Primary Conflict In Human History*, Simon & Schuster, New York: 1987, p. 26.

with others only as a means of collecting and exchanging useful information. Above all, they put a high premium on efficient communication. For that reason, they prefer to communicate with people who transfer information quickly. People who talk too slowly or in general terms are avoided or ignored."

I love the statement of Rex Murphy, the Canadian television commentator and philosopher, in his reference to the paradox of communication and technology, "In this wretched age of super communication, of voice mails, cell phones, beepers, and emails, web sites, help lines and customer service departments, we have never had a greater arsenal of means of communication and no one to talk to!" No truer commentary has been made of recent times.

John O'Neill, a drug and alcohol counselor and director of Menninger Clinic's Professionals in Crisis program in Houston, Texas, treats burned-out business people whose addictions to work and technology have turned them into emotional and physical wrecks.[3] "These are people," says O'Neill, "who check their e-mail several times a minute and are never without their cell phone. They have no boundaries or limits with their work, and two of the tools they use are e-mails and cell phones. They are in touch with the office 24/7, send e-mails at two o'clock in the morning and routinely check office voice mail on vacation. They are chronically needing more minutes on their cellphones and upgrade accordingly... It's like alcohol

47

[3] *The Calgary Herald, November 1st, 2003*

addiction; the more they use it, the more they feel they can't live without it."

O'Neill works with people who never turn their cell phones off. You can spot these people at any resort, upscale hotel, or airport lounge. They use them constantly—at a child's sporting event, at family outings and even when they run marathons! They have to check into the office every opportunity they get, because in their absence they fear the entire business might fade away!

Loneliness and the desire to communicate may indeed be fueling our obsession with cell phones and emails, yet I wonder how connected we really are. You can have a phone number or email address that makes you reachable anywhere in the world any time of the day, but the flipside is an eroding social network that has led to this existential demand for accessibility. In the book *Bowling Alone*, Robert Putman[4] argues that in this era of instant and varied communication, we have become, in fact, more disconnected from friends, family, neighbors, social structures, political parties, and, yes, bowling leagues. This loss of "social capital" is seriously affecting our civic and personal health and putting us in a constant state of anxiety. Simplicity, which was one of the original selling features of technology, is now but an illusion to many who have become slaves to technology. We have allowed technology to take too much from us. Our children, along with ourselves, need to know the naturalness of things—

[4] Cited in *The Calgary Herald*, November 1st, 2003.

beyond the Discovery channel. If we don't help them—and ourselves—experience the sunrise and the stars and the authenticity of nature, simplicity—and life itself—erodes. *Living* images need to be anchored in our consciousness in order to live life both simply and fully, and in order to trust our connection to ourselves and to each other. Entraining to its ever-increasing velocity, many of us have lost our center and have long since forgotten that technology is a tool, not the master.

In his provocative and thought-provoking book, *The Human Factor: Revolutionizing the Way People Live with Technology*, Kim Vincente[5] argues that what our world really needs is technology that works for people. Technological innovation is progressing so quickly that we have fallen behind in our ability to manage it, much less cope with it. He writes, "We are surrounded by objects that invite human error—from VCRs and stoves to operating rooms, airplane cockpits and nuclear power plant control rooms. Problems—some potentially catastrophic—continuously arise when designs are developed without human nature in mind. Our reaction to this dilemma has been to create more sophisticated technology—perpetuating a vicious cycle as we struggle to keep up."

Short of choosing the yogi's path, we are unlikely to eliminate the rhythms of technology and the modern world from our lives. A "return to nature" without technology is not what I am suggesting. I am merely reminding us all that technology is a tool to help us

49

[5] Kim Vincente, *The Human Factor: Revolutionizing the Way People Live with Technology*, Alfred A. Knopf Canada, Toronto, 2003.

create what matters in our life; having been swept about by its elusive power, we are learning to free ourselves of its potential tyranny and put it into perspective in our lives. The rhythms of technology need a counter-balance in our culture, and in each of our lives. Perhaps the antidote is found in the rhythm of a grandmother, as described by an anonymous but very wise nine-year-old...

What is a grandmother?

A grandmother is a lady who has no children of her own. A grandfather is a man grandmother. He goes for walks with the boys and they talk about fishing and tractors and stuff like that.

Grandmothers don't have to do anything except be there. They are old so they shouldn't run or play hard. It's enough if they drive us to the market where the pretend horse is and have lots of quarters ready... They take us for walks. They slow down past things like pretty flowers and caterpillars. And they never say "hurry up..."

Usually grandmothers are fat, but not too fat to tie your shoes. They wear glasses and funny underwear. They can take their teeth and gums off. Grandmothers don't have to be smart. They only have to answer questions like "Why isn't God married?" and "How come dogs chase cats?"

Everyone should try to have a grandmother, especially if you don't have a television. Because they are the only grown-ups who have time.

To become aware of the power of rhythmic entrainment is to take the first step in giving ourselves some options. Sometimes, particularly when we are in achievement mode, we will be entrained with the rhythms of technology and the modern world, and we will need to be. We can also choose, from time to time, to entrain with the rhythms of nature, and love, and connection, and grandmothers. Rather than allowing technology to set the rhythm, use technology to free up time. Then practice using the freed-up time to live the life your heart desires.

Act:

Can you survive one whole day without technological fragmentation and interruption? Are you willing to take the challenge? Book a full day, 24 uninterrupted hours, to conduct this experiment. Invite willing family members or friends to join you. (You will need to schedule a day into your calendar and then honor that scheduled commitment just as you would any other important appointment.)

When the appointed day arrives, turn off the cellular phone, pager, television, DVD player, radio, computer, and any other piece of technology that carries interruption into your life. (Telephone answering machines are our friends in this experiment. So is your car if you use it to get to a favorite spot in nature. If you use it to drive to the mall, you have missed the point entirely!)

This day is about rest, rejuvenation, and fun, but be prepared: it may not be all that easy! Notice how "doing nothing" may feel uncomfortable at first. You may experience some discomfort as you learn to have time for reflection and conversation. Have faith and keep experimenting. Eventually, renewing yourself in this way will help you entrain with a whole new rhythm of creativity, connection, perspective, and a different vision of prosperity.

On a day-to-day basis, you can also simplify your life by creating boundaries around technology:

- Leave your cell phone in the car at night and have periods in the day when you shut it off. Do the same with your computer. Practice being accessible on your terms, not on the tyranny of the urgency of the world's demands.
- Learn to turn off the ringers on phones and computers during times when you are making other, more vital connections with important people in your life. Develop the habit of letting some phones ring in your life without having to answer them just because they are ringing.
- Practice letting go of the need for an instant response to the emails you send people and the messages you leave them on their phones.

two

GUIDEPOSTS AND TEACHERS

We will find freedom once we realize that everything that happens to us has been sent to teach us.

—David Irvine

That First Hard Lesson

The real voyage of discovery consists not in seeking new landscapes, but in having new eyes.

—Marcel Proust

My unique ability to contribute in the world grows from the cross-fertilization of the gifts I was born with and the experiences I have lived. The same is true for you. Some life experiences clearly empower me to contribute in the world, as when the experience of completing a degree in social work enabled me to work as a psychotherapist. Other life experiences will empower me only when I can understand their message. Let me illustrate with a story...

When his sister moved away from home that spring, she gave the little boy her collection of dolls. He carried them carefully to his room, and found each one a special place on his shelves. Sometimes they slept peacefully on his bed. The room was full of every imaginable kind of doll.

One warm summer night the dolls whispered to the boy that they needed houses. A construction project grew which would rival the building of the great pyramids of Egypt, all with Dad's help, of course. Many styles and shapes and colors of houses were lovingly built. It was a grand summer adventure.

That fall, as the leaves turned orange, the boy went to school to begin grade one. He was so excited about all the new friends he would make. School would be such great fun.

One morning, the boy was too rushed to finish his breakfast, and he forgot to comb his hair. He stood in school in front of his new friends and offered his doll collection for "show and tell." At first, silence fell over the classroom. Then the boys in the class began to laugh, and soon the girls joined in. At first the little boy laughed with his friends, but he knew something was wrong. He stopped laughing and looked to his teacher. The teacher looked unhappy. She told the class to be quiet. The little boy quickly returned to his seat and put his dolls away.

After school, the boy ran home without stopping to play. With tears in his eyes, he laid the dolls side by side in a box, and hid the box away. The next morning his mother asked him where his dolls were. The little boy said, "I'm too old to play with dolls now, Mom." He went into his room and closed the door.

As you might suppose, I was the little boy, and that experience was one of my first hard lessons. I didn't know, of course, that my love of dolls might suggest a strong gift for nurturing which would be important later in my life. I certainly didn't predict that the shame I experienced that day would help me to be a better counselor, coach, or teacher, enabling me to understand my clients' fear and shame decades later. I just knew that the other kids did not approve, and that it was time to put the dolls away.

For many years after that day at school, it was not only the doll collection that was disowned and hidden away. I also disowned and hid away a piece of myself. Like many people, and particularly like many of the men that I know, I spent the next twenty years attempting to lock up my feelings. I tried not to be open and nurturing; I tried instead to be closed and strong.

The good news for me was that the story didn't end there. When my parents sold their acreage, more than two decades after that day at school, I went back up to the loft of our old barn and rediscovered all those old dolls. It was a surprisingly joyous reunion. Mostly, I see now, it was a reunion with the nurturing side of myself that I had kept hidden for so long.

Now, many years later, I know that the gift of nurturing is a crucial piece of my unique ability. It makes me a warmer husband, a kinder father, an empathetic consultant, and a more effective business manager. The strong, successful business people I work with have sometimes chosen to hide their nurturing sides. They've bought the same fallacy I did. They've decided that one will undermine the other; that in order to be strong, they can't afford to be nurturing. In reality, people, and businesses, need both. Sometimes we require strength to solve a problem. Sometimes we need to nurture ourselves or others through adversity. I would not understand this in the same way were it not for the catalyst of that first hard lesson.

Reflecting on my childhood experience, I learned that this was not so much a story about dolls, as it was an opportunity to understand how what was important to me as a child is still important to me as an adult. Traumatic experiences can be good teachers. As we follow the thread back to these kinds of experiences, we will often discover they will open the door to help us find our gifts. That experience ultimately opened a door to my soul and invited me to reach inside and discover my true calling. I learned that nurturing others is an integral part of who I am. I also discovered that a piece of my life's purpose is to come closer to the emotional side of myself, and that one of my gifts is to help others do the same. Out of the ashes emerged an awareness of my passion.

I believe all of us possess unique gifts and passions. When our passions, which are often so evident in childhood, get buried in attempts to conform and survive in a world that tells us how we "should" be, we lose touch with our true essence, thus eroding simplicity. In the decades since I recovered that old doll collection, I have taught kindergarten, led scout troops, and worked as a psychotherapist. I foster a sense of community in business organizations through my consultation and workshops. Whenever I remember my doll experience, I am reminded that the passions which we demonstrate as children need to continue to be unwrapped throughout our adult lives.

As we consider the possibilities in initiating or accepting change in our lives, we need to connect with our gifts and experiences. If you are going to reroute your life, however gently, how are you to know which direction to take? The experiences of childhood provide important clues. Try to remember what you enjoyed playing at most when you were young. It doesn't matter if it defied logic. The joy of the moment was real, and the signpost that passion provides is important.

The clearer your connection to your true essence, the closer you come to living a simpler, more contented life. The deeper your understanding of your experiences, the more power you have to use what you have learned. I encourage you to rediscover your lost passions and dreams and experiences. Search for the meaning in your experiences, looking not only with your head, but also with your heart.

Reflect:

Take a trip back in time. Is there an early "hard lesson" you can remember? Perhaps there was an instance where you felt "different"—where you were clearly on the road less traveled and your friends, or those in authority, did not approve. Again, jot down a few notes to help clarify your memory.

Now put a favorite child (perhaps a niece, nephew, grandchild, or friend) into the memory in place of you. What do you see? What unique qualities or passions are being suggested by your "difference?" What would you say to that child about how these unique passions might be further explored?

If this early hard lesson could teach you something about yourself, something that might be important to you today, what would that be?

One Man's Wisdom

A great teacher never strives to explain her vision; she simply invites you to stand beside her and see for yourself.

—The Reverend R. Inman

When I left for college, my father could have offered me the conventional blessing from fathers of his generation. He could have given me a hearty pat on the back and sent me off to achieve "success." The success formula of the day was one which many of my friends received from their fathers: get a marketable education, find a solid company to work for, build a strong financial base, be a good provider. My dad held deep respect for these values, but he was also something of a maverick in his approach to life. He was less traditional in the advice he had to offer. His gifts and experiences had led him to some different conclusions about life, about what is important, about success and meaning.

As far back as I can remember, my varied and sometimes faltering steps on the journey to a meaningful life were inspired and supported by my father. Harlie had his own personal challenges and often suffered from depression, a gift which he genetically passed along as part of my inheritance. From his depression emerged deep wisdom, courage, an ability to connect, and compassion. When I dreamt of making the track and field championships, my dad was my coach. He bought me books on running; he drove me down our farm road and measured the distances; he believed in me when I doubted myself.

My dad had nothing but time for the people he met. There was no such thing as a quick stop with Harlie. He could, and did, visit for a couple of hours at a time with Jake, the man who lived at the garbage dump in our town. Dad could hold people up in a check-out line halfway to forever while he chatted with the cashier. He picked up hitchhikers. He never cared much about being "appropriate." He just loved people.

As a scout leader, dad taught me to survive more than just the physical wilderness. "Ultimate strength," he used to say, "comes from strong roots. Roots are the values that sustain us from the inside. Roots cannot be seen by the world, but they are what's important when the winds of change blow." As he met his challenges over the years, he showed me that strength and nurturing could go hand in hand. I saw in him that it's not the fierceness of the storm that determines whether we break, but rather the strength of the roots which lie below the surface.

The most important value for my dad was to find meaning in life, wherever we are and whatever we do. The university parking lot attendant, who treats each customer with grace and attention because he is representing the university to that customer, would have garnered the respect of my dad. Dad told me that success, as the world measures it, is only a very small piece of the goal. Dad's wish for me was something more subtle and sometimes harder to come by: a life of meaning. He told me that meaning was not something I would find by chance, that I would have to be intentional and it would come to me.

When questioning him further as to his road map for meaning, he offered little, except to encourage me to find my own path, to discover my own unknown frontier of meaning.

"I will give you a few clues, however... remember that great ambition and victory without contribution is without significance. You will have to work diligently, know yourself well, and be ever attentive in your service to others and in your contribution to the world... If you seek meaning," he concluded, "then the yardstick by which the world measures success will not be relevant at all."

Of course, as a youth I had little conscious understanding of the depth of my father's wisdom or the love from which the message originated. Like many young adults, I went off and built a successful life: I graduated from university, got married, created a prosperous business and raised three children. I am grateful for this success, and my father was proud of me in these achievements. He knew, as I now know, that these were important first steps. I established the outward stability of achievement long before I was ready to seek the deeper inner power of connection. But those seeds of his love and his insight were planted, and are taking root, years after his death. Now, after decades of living, I truly appreciate my father's teaching. I understand that outer success is only a piece of the goal. I, too, have become a seeker of meaning.

We all have different experiences of fathers, mothers, and families. Writing about my father carries two risks. One is that I will create a picture of an idyllic, unrealistic father-and-son relationship. I don't want to do that; it would not be true. It takes the clarifying effect of time, and sometimes a lot of time, to understand our parents' teachings. I certainly did not recognize my father's gifts twenty years ago the way I recognize them today; that has taken some personal searching. I have also worked with many clients and colleagues whose parents were, for whatever reason, limited in their ability to nurture, teach, and mentor their children. The second risk in writing about my father, then, is that some readers could discount the rest of my message, because their parents were not like mine.

GUIDEPOSTS AND TEACHERS

The reality is that each of us has special people, somewhere in our lives, who act as our signposts and guides. Parents are one of the possibilities. My father was one of my teachers, but he was not the only one. There have been many others. With all of my teachers, my task has been to understand the lessons being offered. Families and communities can provide the soil to nurture the seed, but inevitably the young tree must set down its own roots to grow and mature. My parents' wisdom helped lay the groundwork for my soul's journey, but the journey has always been mine to explore as I choose.

Reflect:

Take this opportunity to consider the people who have been significant teachers in your life. A good way to capture them all is through a tool given to me by Zig Ziglar, called a "wall of influence." Find photographs of the most important teachers or mentors in *your* life, those who have had a significant impact on you, and mount them on a wall where you will see them often, to remind you of the wisdom, mentoring, and caring that has come your way. You will find, by doing this, that your wall of influence actually becomes a wall of *gratitude* as you reflect upon your heritage and the mentoring afforded to you. You might include parents, other family members, schoolteachers, mentors, early bosses, or important friends. Remember, enormous information is now available and accessible on the Internet. But we need *people*—face-to-face connections with people who care about us—to glean *perspective*, to be *mentored*, and to inherit *wisdom*.

Even if you don't put pictures together, you can capture the essence of the lessons you learned from these people by listing their names on a sheet of paper and writing beside each one your favorite memories and the important lessons you learned from them. There will undoubtedly be memories forgotten and lessons uncovered. You may discover some lessons you are living by that you would rather discard. All are important guideposts on the journey.

Cracking the Dependency Egg

As soon as you know how to trust yourself, you know how to live.

—Goethe

As a child on the farm, I remember watching our neighbor's chicks hatch. The chicks were pecking their way out of their shells, and in an effort to help them I cracked their eggs. To my astonishment, the chicks died. That day, I learned a very important lesson the hard way: help isn't always helpful.

Those chicks needed the struggle of hatching to survive and thrive. They needed to crack their own dependency eggs; they didn't need me to do it for them. I believe the same is true for human beings. If we are to embrace change, if we are to connect with our passions and become more of our true selves, if we are to live a life of meaning, vitality, and eventual contentment, then we will need to identify our dependency eggs, and crack them...

Even as a child, Allan didn't play with the tin trains and tractors his brother enjoyed. His mom would find him out in the barn, building wonderful contraptions out of bits of binder twine, bolts, and lumber. So it was no surprise when he began to pick up the odd handyman job on neighboring farms. Samuel, an old bachelor down the road, spotted the natural talent and taught Allan the art of finishing carpentry.

After a while, Allan moved to the city and joined a cabinet-making company. He followed his manager's advice and went to night school to become a draftsman. Eventually, a drafting position came open, and Allan's manager offered him a promotion to a position in the office. In three years, when the company opened its next branch plant, Allan would be the natural candidate to move into the position of head draftsman.

At the same time, one of Allan's co-workers had a dream of opening his own shop and invited Allan to become his head carpenter. Allan surprised everyone by turning the company promotion down, and going to work for his friend as a master carpenter. "You know, I've been swept along by the conformist tide, never really making my own decisions. And if you don't make your own decisions, they will eventually be made for you. I woke up one morning and found my ladder of success leaning against the wrong wall. I never wanted to push a pencil in an office. I've only ever wanted the feel of wood beneath my hands."

Allan found contentment, and still does, in the art of finishing carpentry.

Our dependency eggs come in many guises. Sometimes we choose a corporate employer that we think will take care of us, and sacrifice our passions and our values along the way. Sometimes we are raised by overly generous parents who rescue us and give more than we need. Perhaps we become accustomed to government programs which we begin to view as a long-term lounge chair instead of a temporary safety net. Maybe we use our health care system to abdicate accountability for our own health. All of these entities—caring employers, generous parents, socially responsible governments, and a strong health care system—are important elements in our society. Sometimes, and for some people, they are essential to survival. For others, however, dependency eggs become hard shells, and we forget that we are meant to be vital and thrive. As Allan discovered, if you don't make your own decisions, eventually they will be made for you.

One aspect of breaking the dependency egg can be our desire as parents or care-givers to over-compensate for our difficult upbringing by forgetting that the way we learned to deal with challenge was by *dealing with it*. In our well-intentioned efforts to create a better future for our children, we can do our kids a disservice by being overly protective. We can also handicap our children by showering them with either excessive safety or possessions without empowering them to learn the valuable lessons of responsibility, work and reward.

I do not want to imply that dependency is bad. We come into this world dependent and we will be dependent all of our lives. The key is to recognize that some kinds of dependency further our growth, while others stifle our development. Accepting accountability is one of the highest forms of human maturity—a willingness to be accountable is one of the defining characteristics and capacities of adulthood. But we do not get there overnight. It is a process, a series of frontiers that must be crossed to experience the necessary strength of mature adulthood. Those who have raised or are raising children know how true this is. A baby, during the first few years of life, through every gesture, movement, and behavior exudes one message to the world: "I am totally dependent on you! I can't do anything for myself, even if I try! I can't be held accountable for the consequences of my choices, after all, I'm just a baby!" Those who care for and influence young children recognize the value of allowing those in our care to depend on us in those early years.

As the years pass and the child reaches adolescence, the message will be very different. It will sound something like this: "Why don't you just leave me alone! I can handle my life and make my own choices. I want to be totally *in*dependent! I don't want to accept any accountability for anything beyond my own very clearly well defined needs and desires." Fighting for independence, as difficult as this stage is, is a needed juncture along the journey to mature adulthood.

It's only when we have at last grown up that the first two messages: "I'm totally dependant on you" *and* "I'm totally independent of you," finally turn into inter-dependence: *"You can depend on me, and I can depend on you,"* which is the mature adult outlook of life. The interdependence stance can help us differentiate the dependencies that support our growth and those that suffocate us.

Allowing our children to break their dependency eggs as they grow is not easy. Yet overdoing for children in an overly controlling, protecting, or dominating adult environment will never allow them the chance to develop their own resources. I remember my mother telling me stories of how, in grade one in 1928, she rode her horse six miles—across railroad tracks—to get to school. She was scared, but as she was often forced to figure things out on her own, she developed a sense of self-esteem and independence. In the timeless wisdom of her later years, she would often speak to me of the value of giving our children space to figure things out on their own, to trust them and not to over-protect them. By having to face unfamiliar situations, we access inner abilities and resources we otherwise would never have realized. "The real danger today," she used to say, "is not what children may encounter on their way to school, but in not allowing them to develop their capacity to courageously face new challenges."

73

Even though I respected my mother's wisdom and perspective, I argued with her then that "these times are not the same. There are new dangers that children face today that we must protect them from!" Yet, as both I and my children mature, I begin to settle in to a deeper understanding of what she was trying to say. Just as her father took the time to explain the dangers of their day, of the hazards and solutions of crossing a railroad track or of dealing with the many mishaps that can come with farm life, so, too, must we prepare our children, in the spirit of love *and* trust, to deal with the potential mishaps of living in our world, without the continual protection of an adult. We will not always be there and if we don't teach our children to deal with life without us present, when will they ever learn?

At a practical level, we can teach our children about the lures of a potential abductor just as we teach them about dealing with the tons of steel we call automobiles, moving swiftly on our city streets. But our teaching must go beyond the naïve response, "Don't talk to strangers." The issue is not strangers, for how will they ever trust the world, much less make friends, if they never talk to strangers? Just as they must learn to stop, look and listen before crossing a street, so, too, must they learn to trust and distinguish a bad stranger from a good stranger.

Above all, we have to teach our children two vital principles. First, to trust their instincts. "If you listen to your heart, I mean *really* listen," I tell my children, "you will be able to tell a safe adult from an adult who may hurt you. If in any doubt whatsoever, if you ever feel something is not right, *trust yourself* to get away from that situation and come and find us or an adult that you know you can trust."

Second, as we prepare children as best we can for the dangers of the present-day world, we must keep hold of our own inner stability as care-givers and help our children remember that the world, with all its dangers, is still a good place to live in. We must remind ourselves and those in our care that most adults are safe and good, and surround them with a community of grown-ups that reinforce this. There is, in fact, no documented increase in child abduction today, but only a perceived increase due, in part, to increased media accessibility and attention.

Like the fear of terrorists, we lose the war against the potential risk to our children when we make choices based on unreasonable fear. We conquer terrorism, just as we triumph over those who could harm our children, when we choose faith, and instill confidence and trust in our children.

In our culture most of us are looking for a life of comfort, safety, and predictability. Yet life is a developmental process. We are always growing and changing. In preparing our children for the realities of stepping out into an unpredictable world, we must remember that all growth requires risk. Minimize risk and we stifle growth.[1] There is a delicate balance between growing our children up too fast, and never allowing

[1] I am grateful for the thought-provoking and stimulating conversation I had my sister, Kate Harling, in the development of this chapter. Her wisdom, sage advice, and presence remain a strength and support in my life.

them to grow up. Children need time to be children, to be held in the nurturing lap of a caring parent. It is vital to make your child's early life as predictable, safe, and loving as possible. And, out of well-meaning and loving concern, we must be careful not to make life too easy for our young people as they grow and develop. Perhaps we need to view our children as hatching chicks and allow them to experience the struggles of life, at the same time as we support, trust and challenge them along the way.

In order to prevent the over protection of those dependent on us, we first must take an honest look at how, as adults, we use crutches that stifle our own growth toward maturity. The challenge is to see the dependencies in our own lives that prevent us from the authentic growth and sustained contentment we are capable of. Anyone who has struggled with an addiction and has gone through the darkness and tortures of the damned, courageously met it, lived through it, and found freedom in the recovery journey, knows one of the great triumphs of human existence.

Take, for example, Fresh I E (Ron Wilson), a Winnipeg rapper nominated in the 46th Grammy Awards, for his CD, *Red Letterz*, for Best Gospel Rock Album. Ron Wilson grew up in Winnipeg's north end. His mother was a prostitute and Ron saw things he said no child should ever have been exposed to. He became addicted to alcohol and street drugs. At the time, his nickname was "Freshie."

He cracked his dependencies through both a miracle and through courage. He said his pastor told him he would hear from God. One day Ron saw a blind man trying to cross the street. He yelled at him to stay put until the traffic cleared, and then told him when he could safely cross. Later that day, Ron came home, where he saw a crowd of people standing outside his residence. He went to the window to ask them why they were there. They were looking at the blind man who was now sitting on Ron's steps.

Ron began to think that if a man can make it through life without eyes, what did this tell him about the way *he* was living? He and the blind man talked. Ron courageously faced his dependencies and, one day at a time, overcame his addiction to alcohol, cigarettes, and street drugs. In his words, he "detoxicated" his body. He became a new person in the process of breaking free from these anesthetizing dependencies while finding renewed dependencies that helped, rather than hindered, his growth. He eventually could not even bring himself to swear or think hostile thoughts. He is now married with children and is working to take his story to youth. His nickname now: Fresh I E—which stands for Fresh in Eternity.

Ron Wilson is a brave example of my premise that we are not the product of our upbringing; rather we are the product of the *choices* we make in our upbringing. When we trade dependency and the illusion of security for personal fulfillment and a life of meaning, we have made a hard choice with grave consequences to our soul.

On the flip side, when we enable someone else to stay in a position of destructive dependency, we are helping to rob them of personal choice and subsequent accountability, well-intentioned or not.

Again, I am not implying here that dependency in every form is wrong. We are born dependent, and will, to a degree, be dependent all our lives. The key is to pay attention—to recognize when our dependencies are imprisoning us, when we are using dependencies to keep us from being fully present or fully alive and when we need to crack our own dependency eggs.

The real payoff of supporting people to take responsibility for their lives is not the financial or worldly success that may come to them as a result of your stepping back. The lasting reward is the quality of character you develop along the way. Consider the story of a young man who had a very old and rich uncle. When the uncle died the young man was called to the office of his attorney and told that he was left a huge fortune. To collect it, however, he was instructed that he first had to run a certain errand, which was described on a slip of paper. It seemed simple enough, but when the young man tried to accomplish the task, the first undertaking turned into another and another and then another. As he pursued his uncle's final requests the young man was led into foreign lands, exotic adventures, and untold dangers. More years passed and the young man nearly lost track of how or even why he was on this long journey, and he could hardly imagine what his end might be. At last, the odyssey led him back into the very same lawyer's office from whence his journey had begun.

"I am here to collect my inheritance," said the heir, no longer a young naïve boy, but now a much wiser, stronger, more confident man.

The lawyer smiled and replied, "As your uncle intended, you have already collected your inheritance, by the experiences you have had, the values you gleaned, and the wisdom you have gained ... And again, as he intended, this inheritance will last you for a lifetime."[2]

Struggle allows the young to trust themselves by investing themselves in the process of life and develop that most valuable of character traits—personal maturity. The words of Mahatma Ghandhi come to mind here in reference to what he explained as the seven deadly sins that would bring destruction to an individual, and eventually to a society:

1. Wealth without work
2. Pleasure without conscience
3. Knowledge without character
4. Commerce without morality
5. Politics without principles
6. Science without humanity
7. Religion without sacrifice

---

[2] With appreciation to Jim Rohn, in his audio tape, *Cultivating An Unshakeable Character*, for this story of the uncle and the inheritance.

Success that comes too easily or too quickly almost never lasts. For those who achieve this kind of success there is always a loitering feeling that they haven't really earned it, and this feeling will eat away at their character, the foundation of self-trust.

Learning to let go, to break free of dependency, and to trust ourselves, does not happen all at once. It is necessary, along the way, to become aware of the ways in which dependency might be blocking us from something more important. The means to cracking that dependency will come in time. When we have begun the initial struggle for self-sufficiency—cracking the egg so to speak—we can continue the journey toward contentment by coming to know ourselves in our achievements and in our connections.

We cannot grow into interdependence and maturity in a controlled environment, trying to make the world safe, secure and predictable, either for ourselves or for others. We will ultimately fail at that task. The external world will never provide enough certainty for us to feel certain, or enough safety for us to feel safe. Safety, security, and ultimately contentment, can only be found from within. I end this chapter with the words of Helen Keller, who wrote so eloquently about the illusion of security in the external world:

"Security is mostly a superstition; it does not exist in nature, nor do the children of men as a whole experience it. Avoiding danger is no safer in the long run than outright exposure. Life is either a daring adventure or nothing!"

Reflect and Act:

Are there any places in your life where you are stuck inside a shell of dependency? What are the old attitudes and fears that keep you overly dependent on others? What do you personally need to become more vital and free? Think of some activities where you can develop courage and personal confidence by acting independently. This can happen in small steps. You might choose to go to a movie by yourself, or take yourself out to dinner. Maybe it is time for something bigger: to try living on your own, or taking a vacation by yourself, or looking for a new and more rewarding job, or creating your own employment.

Look carefully at the disparaging dependencies in your own life that impede your growth—be they alcohol, damaging relationships, work environments and habits, food, prescription drugs—and are keeping you anesthetized from facing yourself and robbing your of your freedom. Remember, without freedom, there will be no space for contentment or simplicity. Take a good look at yourself, and how you may have become a slave to these potential addictions. Find a recovery program and the path to freedom.

On the flip side, consider whether you are helping someone stay stuck in their own shell of dependency. Is it possible that your "help" is not really "helping?" Do you need to practice some "tough love" and make space for someone in your life to crack the dependency egg?

The Heroic Journey

*We cannot do great things on this earth. We can
only do little things with great love.*

—Mother Teresa

Joseph Campbell, the renowned twentieth century
scholar on comparative mythology, connects myths
from a wide range of cultures and periods of human
history. In 1949, he published his masterful work, *The
Hero with a Thousand Faces*. One of the profound
teachings of this book is the concept of the "hero's
journey," which I think of as the path of courageous
personal change. According to Campbell, the journey is
comprised of three elements. First, the hero is challenged by a call to adventure, an adventure which will
require some form of separation, loss, or change. Next,
in choosing to respond to this call, the hero is faced
with obstacles and ordeals on the path of initiation into
something new. Finally, the hero is transformed, the

"something new" is integrated, and the journey ends at a place of victory or new life.

Joseph Campbell's work deals with the enduring patterns of change that occur to people over and over again as they pursue their own individual heroic journeys. The hero's journey has been told and retold in countless stories old and new. In George Lucas' movie *Star Wars*, inspired by Joseph Campbell, the character of Luke Skywalker epitomizes this heroic quest. Luke receives the call to embrace a mission beyond the scope of his understanding. He finds the courage to leave the comforts of home, and embarks on an adventurous journey into the unknown. He seeks to experience a force greater than himself, a force which requires him to challenge the dark side and triumph over evil. Young Skywalker uncovers the painful truth about his past, and yet he goes on to transform himself and his community out of his faith, trust, and courage. The patterns are relevant to other modern heroic journeys such as *Lord of the Rings*, as well as to older classics from the *Odyssey* to *Pilgrim's Progress*.

The first step in the hero's journey is listening for and heeding the call to adventure. We have talked about calls to change, the big dramatic wake-up calls, the small personal nudges of discomfort, the powerful inner desire for a life of meaning. We know that we are unlikely to hear the call, or feel capable of responding, unless we examine the pace of our lives. We also know that change is a constant; the one thing we can count on is that there will be a call. Someone offers us a glimpse of a potentially fulfilling journey. Something stops us dead in the tracks of our current path. However the challenge arises, we all have the opportunity to become the hero.

When we are ready for the adventure—or when we can't stand our old ways for one more day—we take some action to change. Now we step into the stage of struggle and chaos, and more courage. Perhaps we will be required to go seven times into battle...

Robert the Bruce, the Scottish tribal leader, had gone into battle six times in an attempt to unify the tribes of Scotland. Every time he had failed. Following the last failure he retreated, deserted by his soldiers and alone, to a small hut deep in the mountains. In the hut was one solitary piece of furniture, an old table adjacent to the single small window. Bruce was sitting on the floor in a corner, huddled into his cloak against the cold, and empty of hope, when a lone spider traveling the windowsill caught his eye. The spider made a seemingly impossible leap from the windowsill toward the table. It missed and fell to the floor.

Because he had nothing else to do (being a totally defeated man) Bruce continued to watch the spider as it scuttled across the floor, crawled up the wall to the window sill, and leapt for the table again. Again it missed and fell. Again it went back to the wall. Bruce followed it through four more missed attempts. Finally, on the seventh try, the spider barely made it across to the top of the table. And as a weak shaft of sunlight entered the room, Bruce realized that the spider, in the process of struggling, had actually begun to spin its web.

Bruce contemplated what he had just witnessed, the adversity, the tenacity, and the inevitable achievement, unseen though it was in the midst of the action. As he considered this demonstration, Bruce began to wonder why he himself should give up on his dream, his vocation, his call to adventure.

A short time later, empowered by the teaching of one small spider, he ventured forth to find the allies and build the plans to go back into battle yet once again. Only this time he won, and succeeded in forging Scotland into a new nation, with he, Bruce, as its first king.

Robert the Bruce was in the struggle and anguish of his heroic journey for a long time: discouraged, defeated, quitting, learning, going back for one more round. This is a difficult—and necessary—phase of growth. Chaos is a natural state in the process of change. As we step off the edge of stability, we will need to let go of the comfort of the familiar. Loss, insecurity, fear, and uncertainty always precede new growth. Letting go is never easy. We have seen in the stories we have shared that responding to the call may require a shift in our attachments: to a particular career path, to an income level, to a familiar perception of ourselves, or to the approval we receive from others. The greater our attachments, the harder it is to let go, and the greater the degree of chaos we will experience.

This is why it is also true that before things get better, they will often get worse. Ironically, the more we fight chaos, the longer it lasts. The buoyancy principle definitely applies here. When you are drowning, or sinking in quicksand, the more you fight it, the worse it gets. In chaotic times, it is crucial to let go and allow yourself to float with the waves. The chaos stage will end. You just can't hurry it up by panicking.

A great future awaits us, in our inner connection and in our outer achievement, if we seek to be our truest selves and take the heroic journey. We can reach the place of integration, victory, and transformation. I cannot tell you what the steps will be, or how long they will take, or how many detours are waiting; as Joseph Campbell said, these are the things each of us must sort out for ourselves. What I do know is that we live in a society that values and adores those of celebrity status, while often undermining the worth of small— and vital—contributions. Collectively, we applaud and revere the elite athletes, the famous entertainers, the successful entrepreneurs, the Everest climbers, the billionaires, and, to a lesser extent, the Nobel Prize winners. We are in awe of anyone who has attained fame, notoriety, and celebrity status, especially if they have overcome a devastating misfortune to reach the pinnacle of their dreams and their vocation. Indeed, I am inspired by the stories of successful people who follow their passion and perhaps even their calling and manifest their destiny by pushing the boundaries of possibilities to their outermost limits. There is, without doubt, a time and a place for great achievements. For the past twenty years I have dedicated my life to the growth of a successful business in personal and organizational development and the subsequent contribution this business has made to the world. I have trained hard for competitive marathon racing. I have found great pride in my ambitions and in my accomplishments.

I also acknowledge the inspiration in the stories of so many achievers that have walked before me, but I am now reaching a point in my life where I am finding increasing value in simply being and doing good work, with or without fame. I am increasingly respectful of the hundreds of people I meet each year who will never achieve fame or recognition by the world's standards and who quietly and steadily go about their lives every day, volunteering in their community, standing tall on their inner convictions in the face of the culture, painting an unsigned masterpiece, recovering from an addiction, lying beside a parent while they die, or compassionately holding a loved one who is coming to terms with a terminal illness.

Recently, a staff member at a long-term care facility in our city was brutally murdered in her apartment. In life she made a difference simply by being ordinary and doing ordinary work. At her memorial service, over two hundred people crowded into the atrium to say farewell. Friends, colleagues, and residents spoke of her warm smile, bright eyes, and the quiet way she went about helping the residents.

While this woman was not famous and led quite an ordinary life, she was special in how she approached her work and others—and consequently made a big difference in many people's lives.

In the summer of 2003, a community in central British Columbia, Canada, saw 30,000 people—almost one-third of Kelowna—forced from their homes by the wind-driven Okanagan Mountain Provincial Park fire. In all, 238 homes would burn. It was hard to image things getting worse, until Kelowna Fire Chief Gerry Zimmermann took a call from Platoon Capt. Len Moody. The inferno had roared past, trapping fire crews and forcing the rest to regroup at Kelowna's southern edge. Moody warned that the very road they were on could fall, leaving the city at risk. They agreed they might have to bulldoze a neighborhood to save the city.

"My heart thumped a couple of times," Zimmermann said. He asked operations staff to plot a fireguard and assemble heavy equipment. "There was such trust no one raised an eyebrow," he says. They were within an hour of flattening homes when the winds died down. Meanwhile, crews cut off by flames continued battling house fires, uncertain of their own fate. Zimmerman would learn later that among those trapped firefighters was his twenty-six-year-old son, Chris.[1]

Two months after the fires, I spoke to Kelowna's business community. With the tragedy and shock of

89

[1] MACLEAN'S, December 29th, 2003, pages 22-23

the fire still so close to their community and to the consciousness of every one of its citizens, we took time that day to step back and reflect on the experience. It was acknowledged within this group that the healing, the transformation, and the coming together of the community was due, to a huge degree, to the leadership of their fire chief, Gerry Zimmerman. There were several unsolicited comments that day expressing admiration for their fire chief—their hero who led them through the fire that summer.

When asked, "What were the leadership qualities that earned your respect and trust for him?" the responses were related to the strength of his authentic presence. "His realness, his vulnerability, and his humility," were a small summary of the comments expressed that day. "For many, the chief's daily fire briefings embodied the spirit of Kelowna. His blunt assessments came unfiltered. His emotions were like turbulent weather: occasional tears, with flashes of outrage, followed by gales of laughter."[2]

Kelowna is rebuilding, but it will take time. Zimmerman, like so many others, believes that the city and the department have emerged stronger. *"We've learned how important people are—not things,"* he said.

Zimmerman has accepted a long list of speaking engagements and fundraisers from clubs, aid agencies, and churches. "It is a chance to repay those who helped. The attention is flattering, but this was a 'massive group effort,'" he says. "It was about *thousands* of

[2] Ibid.

people—I just happened to be the one who got to talk about it from time to time."

The strength of Gerry's leadership capacity came from his own personal heroic journey. He learned humility, the value of openness, the strength of vulnerability, and the capacity of the human spirit, in part, through the death of his wife in a car crash seven years earlier. "It helped prepare me," he said, "for what I went through here." On his journey, he found his own refuge on his hobby farm where his children were raised.

Deservedly, Zimmerman was named, by *Maclean's* magazine, as one of their "Canadians of the Year" in 2003. Yet, I think that the respected and humble Gerry Zimmerman would tell us all that it is not the reward or the public recognition that ever really matters in the true hero's journey. Many of these contributors to society today will never get a gold medal, a platinum CD, or an Oscar nomination for the lives they have touched and changed. They, like so many who quietly serve their communities with their presence and their gifts, won't get into any "hall of fame" or receive a Nobel prize for the passion and energy they bring to their work and their lives every day, in spite of their weariness and the demands placed upon them. Most of the true heroes in our society go unnoticed by society's standards. They will never get recognition in the press for their dedicated day-in and day-out contribution to the lives of their communities or families. For many, the rewards are nothing more than a meaningful, fulfilled life that comes from contribution, from the commitment to make the world a better place through their presence.

I think that what each of us seeks is the fulfillment of our own potential. Where there is a path, it is someone else's way. Whenever we are faced with difficulty, there is an opportunity for a heroic journey. Listen to the heart call that beckons us to develop our unique gifts. Transform that creative drive into action. In the words of the great dancer and choreographer, Martha Graham:

"There is a vitality, a life force, a quickening, that is translated through you into action, and because there is only one of you in all time, this expression is unique. If you block it, it will never exist through any other medium, and it will be lost. The world will not have it. It is not your business to determine how good it is, nor how valuable it is, nor how it compares with any other expressions. It is your business to keep it yours, clearly and directly, to keep the channel open. You have to keep open and aware, directly, of the urges that motivate you."

The heroic journey beckons. The road map to fulfillment and contentment lies within.

Reflect:

The heroic journey begins with a call to change. Use one or all of the following questions to help you hear the call in your life. This is a good time for unedited "brainstorm writing." No inner critique, no judgment, no fear, no rules!

Ask yourself, "What are my passions?" and "Why is it that I lose track of time when I am engaged with one of my passions?"

Begin to understand your life purpose by reflecting on these questions. Why do you get out of bed in the morning? What would you want people to say about you after you die? If you didn't have to earn a living, what would you choose to do to contribute in your community?

three

CONNECT

"When I was young and free and my imagination had no limits, I dreamed of changing the world; as I grew older and wiser I discovered the world would not change, so I shortened my sights somewhat and decided to change my country, but it too seemed immovable. As I grew into my twilight years, in one last desperate attempt, I settled for changing only my family, those closest to me. But alas, they would have none of it!

And now I realize as I lie on my death bed, if I had only changed myself first, then, by example, I might have changed my family. From their aspirations and encouragement I would have then been able to better my country, and who knows, I might have even changed the world."

—Inscribed at the tomb of an Anglican Bishop in
  Westminster Abbey

Opening a Door

Productive work, love and thought are possible only if the person can be, when necessary, quiet and alone. To be able to listen to oneself is the necessary condition for relating oneself to others.

—Erich Fromm

As we considered the need for change a few chapters ago, I talked about the rhythms of life, especially the rhythms of technology and of grandmothers. Since we cannot take the journey to deeper contentment without altering the pace of our lives, I want to reflect a little more about pace and rhythm and speed. The truth here is absolutely simple. The journey towards contentment begins by slowing down.

It is also absolutely true that slowing down is a simple concept which most of us find quite difficult to practice. Once again, let me offer a real life story...

Richard built a successful company from the bottom up. He created the income necessary to treat his family to travel and adventure. Every year he planned a family dream vacation, and every year his family flew off to exotic locations while he stayed behind to run his company. Finally, after years of tearful and frustrating farewells, Richard agreed to hire a manager and he escaped with his wife and three children to the sandy beaches of the South Pacific.

The first day, Richard lay in the sun and wondered how the new manager was coping while his children snorkeled in the crystal waters.

The second day, Richard paced in the roaring surf and slipped back to his room in mid-afternoon to place a long-distance phone call and check on business.

The third day, Richard stayed behind in the restaurant and poured over the financial section of an international newspaper. He called the office twice before noon.

The fourth day, Richard couldn't take it anymore. He left his family behind in tropical paradise and flew back home to the comfortable routine of "busyness."

Many of us will recognize a version of our own lives in Richard's story. Our thoughts and energies are consumed by work; we have become entrenched in the rhythm of achievement and busyness, and we know no other. The rhythm of connection, at least at the beginning, is foreign, and often uncomfortable, boring, and difficult to find. What would you say if I asked you to add up, for the past year, or the past week, or yesterday, how much time you took for genuine relaxation, for simply being?

The rhythm of connection, with ourselves and with others, requires a conscious shift to a pace which is more personal. First, of course, we will have to learn what that personal pace is. We will need to create room in our lives—physical, mental, emotional, and spiritual room—to notice our own internal rhythms. Perhaps we will need to walk at a different rate than usual, or stop in a park on the way home from work, or sit and listen to Mozart at the beginning or the end of the day. Many downtown churches and synagogues in our community are starting to leave their doors open at lunchtime, and business people are finding a quiet place for personal contemplation and slowing down. Each of us will know what works for us, or we can experiment until we find out. We will also need to remember that it is difficult to appreciate our own rhythms when we regularly choose the rhythm of television, radio, or the Internet for company.

One of the most important ways we can begin to slow down, to seek the rhythm of inner connection by easing ourselves away from the rhythm of achievement, is through daily quiet time or silence. A routine of daily quiet time can begin by finding a space somewhere where silence could be an option. This might be the balcony, the basement, the nearest park bench, or your favorite chair in the living room. (If you have as many people living in your home as we have in ours, this may also require headphones, ear plugs, a soundproof fire door, or some creative scheduling.) Whatever space you choose, make it your personal sanctuary, at least for a few minutes every day. You may want to give some thought to the decor. Are there pictures, books, or other personal items you can place in this space, objects that will bring a sense of peace and calm?

When I started the practice of taking daily quiet time, it was first a discipline. Then it became a habit. Now it is a gift. I once heard that when asked how he was able to accomplish so much in his lifetime, Mahatma Gandhi replied, "The way that I am able to accomplish so much is that I meditate two hours a day, unless I am very busy, and then I meditate four hours a day." Just as it is vital to the body to be nourished by the practice of regular, healthy meals, so, too, is it vital to the mind and spirit to make time daily to be nourished by the practice of quiet time. If you want the good in you to grow, you must bring it out of the darkness of our busy, frantic lives and into the sunlight of the spirit. Making time to be still is a step out into the sun.

In the sanctuary I have created in which to take my quiet time I have a comfortable chair and cushion. The sanctuary is simple, nothing fancy or elaborate. I surround myself with pictures, images, photos, and mementos that are meaningful to me, that help bring me back to myself, my spiritual nature, and help me connect with the divine within me. My quiet time is an interconnected practice of self-assessment, meditation, and prayer. I may start my quiet time by simply tuning in to myself. If I need to relax, I imagine myself on a favorite beach and breathe deeply, allowing my body to calm down. Then I notice where I carry tension in my body and breathe in the healing and relaxing sunlight that surrounds me. If I find my mind wandering, as it usually does, I gently bring myself back to my breathing, back to the beach in my mind, by putting my thoughts on a log or raft, and watch them drift out to sea.

Meditation is simply and practically a way of quieting my mind so that I can be receptive to a power greater than myself. I may simply contemplate the plants in my sanctuary, and the magnificent power of creation behind the manifestation of a simple plant. I may focus on my feelings, or ask myself, "What is my busyness today taking me away from? What is going on in my life?" Sometimes, if I am in need of wisdom, I will picture having a conversation with my mother, my father, or a wise person in my life whom I respect and wish to learn from. I find that my relationship with both my parents has actually deepened since their death. After all, there is no baggage to deal with when you connect to someone spiritually. Both my parents have become important guides from beyond.

Patience is a vital requirement in the development of a contemplative life. As we learn to listen to the voice within, it takes time to distinguish passing feelings and short-lived impulses from deeper guidance and perspective. As you develop the art and skill of listening to a voice beneath the surface of your mind, it is easy to confuse emotions or impulsive thoughts with intuition. You may, for example, be going through a period in your life when you are feeling some general discontentment, but do not know precisely what is at the root of it. After spending a few minutes in meditation or prayer, you suddenly get a feeling that all of your problems are caused by your stressful job or difficult boss and that you should immediately quit and find a new career. Although this scenario is undoubtedly an extreme example, it illustrates that going within and listening for deeper truth is very distinct from allowing fleeting whims and impulsive emotions to direct our decisions. Wisdom and direction from within does not usually come in a momentary blinding burst, but rather in a gradual awakening brought about by the practice of daily prayer and meditation.

What I discover, as I continue the practice day after day, is that I may not always be uplifted or clear, or completely relaxed after every reflective period. However, as I reflect back over my life in recent years since commencing a daily contemplative practice, I sense a deeper trust in myself and in life itself. After doing this day after day, I gain guidance, clarity, and inner peace and feel more relaxed and confident.

More important than having a space, and more difficult for most of us, is the need to commit your time. You may want to try getting up a bit early, using a piece of your lunch hour, or taking some time before dinner or bed. For most of us, that's the hardest part; we wouldn't need to slow down if we didn't have a demanding schedule to slow down from. Or perhaps it has been our habit to break the rhythm of business with a couple of hours in front of the television. This allows us to withdraw from achievement, but it will not move us toward connection. Despite the obstacles, I know a little time every day can truly work a miracle. Meditate, pray, or simply relax. The goal here is nothing more than to slow down the everyday chatter of the mind.

This reflective, contemplative time is very personal and unique for each individual. No prescription can be given as to how to use your quiet time "effectively." The important thing is to make this time set aside for stillness both meaningful and personal to you. Like a muscle that may need developing in your life, stay with it, even through the boredom or the judgment that it is "wasting time." Your capacity to sit still and access your inner wisdom will be strengthened over time. Quiet times have been a tremendous gift to me, a time for renewal and rejuvenation. It is a restorative time, a place of quieting the noise of my day-to-day life. But they are not always that way. Sometimes they are just an anxious time of sitting and waiting for my thirty minutes to be up. But I just keep doing it, and the muscle gets stronger.

I used to work like crazy and then rest like crazy. The more my work and activity was manic, the harder I would crash at the end of the week or month or year. The crash would come in the form of getting sick on holidays, migraine headaches on the weekends, depression in the slow, periods, or, at minimum, anxiety and discomfort when I took any time off. My slowing-down time was in big blocks: two weeks at a cabin, or a week of solo camping in the mountains, or an intensive weekend of silence at a local retreat center. Slowing down on vacations or taking mini-holidays is great, but for me the work-like-crazy/rest-like-crazy pattern became a personal rhythm of all-or-nothing extremes. Slowing down a little every day has developed into an achieve/connect rhythm which allows me to be more effective in all aspects of my life, every day of the year. Daily reflection does not take the place of a good vacation, but neither does a good vacation replace daily reflection time.

Just as connection with self requires sensitivity to our own rhythms, connection with others requires sensitivity to theirs. The most rewarding relationships, whether spouse to spouse, parent to child, or friend to friend, are those in which we can comfortably entrain with one another's rhythms. Without question, this is going to be difficult in the midst of too much achievement-oriented activity. We will need to explore the means by which we can become aware of, and learn to appreciate, the rhythms of the people with whom we share our lives.

Slowing down truly is opening a door to the soul. When we commit to and honor the time for quiet personal reflection, our lives will begin to change almost without further effort. Paradoxically, we will become more connected to our friends and families as we begin to experience some inner peace. We will become less susceptible to stress, mood swings, or any form of escape. Through personal quiet time, we create the possibility that contemplation and self-knowledge will become our foundations for action. Then, rather than continuously reacting to outside stimuli, we can consciously steer our lives in the direction of the soul's choosing.

Act to Reflect:

Instead of reading about the experience of quiet time, let's actually experience quiet time. Advise anyone who is likely to interrupt you that you need ten more minutes. Turn down the lights, put your feet up, take a few slow, deep breaths, and close this book. As much as you can, set aside thoughts of to-do lists and urgent tasks. If you fall asleep, you probably need the rest. Whatever your experience, save ten minutes out of tomorrow's schedule (eventually try to work up to twenty to thirty minutes) and try again. Allow some personal peace to sneak into a corner of your mind and soul.

Sometime this week, stake out some private physical space for regular contemplation. Simple living calls us to create a sanctuary in our lives, a place of shelter and refuge from the demands of the world, a place we can go within, to be able to sit comfortably and in quiet. A spare bedroom, a cozy corner of your basement, a spot on the porch, a favorite park—use what you have. Do at least one thing to make your chosen space inviting to you. Perhaps you need to add a footstool, a comforter, or a candle. You may want to surround yourself with

105

images, pictures, and photographs that inspire and support you to rest, renew, and refocus on what matters most. If you are seeking privacy outside, headphones and some gentle music can do wonders. If you are seeking calm in the midst of a busy family or active roommates, protect your peace with a pair of ear plugs!

Stewardship and the Compassionate Heart

I sought my God, and my God I could not see;
I sought my soul, and my soul eluded me;
I sought to serve my brother in his need and
found all three:
My God, my soul, and thee.

—Anonymous

The journey to connect with our truest selves is always going to be incomplete, until we take what we have learned and share it in the world. Remember the yogi in the story of the yogi and the businessman, possibly isolated in contemplation and perhaps unable to build meaningful connections with others. Our goal is not to stop at self-reflection; we seek to create a life of deeper integration. This means we take the time daily for contemplation, for quietness, for time to listen to a deeper side of ourselves and then bring this new awareness to the world in the service of others.

A few years ago I had reached a crossroads in my career. On my days off, I was feeling a sense of exhaustion, not the "good" tired that comes from wholehearted weariness, but the "bad" tired that comes from misalignment. Even though my work was paying the bills, it wasn't feeding my soul. Something was missing and I couldn't quite get a handle on it. I made a conscious choice to resist my tendency to push these uncomfortable emotions aside and just keep busy. I knew, from past experience, that doing so would simply lead to more sleepless nights and increased anxiety. After all, the feelings have to come out somewhere.

This time I decided to go through the discomfort of facing my inner self. I took extra time during the week to walk my dog, to sit by the river, to simply be with myself. It wasn't a lot of time, just an extra hour or two after lunch to get out of the house and reflect. Some of that contemplative time was unfocused, as I allowed myself to "feel" my discomfort, and to "feel" the beauty that surrounded me. Over time, a renewed self began to emerge. I looked back to my deep desires as a child. I remembered the doll story and my forgotten interest in relationships. As I began remembering the impact people have had in my life, I recalled a conversation with my mother, and how she had pointed out it was my gift to work at the heart level. I came to the realization that much of the work I was doing was misaligned with my gift of the heart. Vulnerability is one of my greatest strengths, and yet, much of my work meant pushing my heart aside as I helped organizations with their performance management and strategic planning processes. That year I became determined to align my work with my deepest values and my unique talents.

As I took steps to integrate my inner desires with my achievements in the outside world, I began to uncover the value of taking my gifts out into the light. I believe an important guiding principle on this leg of the journey is the compassionate heart, lived out in acts of stewardship.

Stewardship is about following the thread of our passions, our soul's desires, to find our gifts and then to hold ourselves accountable for allowing these gifts, whatever they are, to flow into our community. It is about sharing our gifts with our loved ones. The life-giving power of authentic giving is beautifully illustrated by Bruce Barton in this parable...

There are two seas in Palestine. One is fresh, and fish live in it. Splashes of green adorn its banks. Trees spread their branches over it and stretch out their thirsty roots to sip of its healing waters. Along its shores the children play. The river Jordan flows into this sea with sparkling water from the hills. So it laughs with sunshine. Men build their houses near it, and birds their nests, and every kind of life is happier because the sea is there.

Then the river Jordan flows on south into another sea.

Here there is no splash of fish, no fluttering leaf, no song of birds, no children's laughter. Travelers choose another route, unless they are on urgent business. The air hangs heavy above its waters; man, beast, and bird will not drink from it.

What makes this mighty difference between these neighbor seas? Not the river Jordan; it empties the same good water into both. Not the soil in which they lie, not the country about. This is the difference. The Sea of Galilee receives but does not keep the Jordan. For every drop that flows into it, another drop flows out. The giving and receiving go on in equal measure. The other sea is shrewder, hoarding its income jealously. It will not be tempted into any generous impulse. Every drop it gets, it keeps. The Sea of Galilee gives and lives. The other sea gives nothing. It is named the Dead Sea.

Stewardship, the way of the compassionate heart, allows the goodness of life to flow. When we live from the place of stewardship, there is no division between giving and receiving: when we give, we receive, and when we receive, we give. This is not always a back-and-forth process; sometimes we receive from some, and we give to others. In the process, we trade our feelings of lonely rootlessness for a sense of belonging to a human community greater than ourselves.

A while ago, I was traveling in a northern community to speak to a group of people who spend their summers fighting forest fires. I was picked up at the airport by a former first aid instructor, a wonderful, lively man with a down-to-earth philosophy of life. He told me the three most important words you can offer when you come upon an accident victim are, "Can I help?"

This simple phrase started me thinking about the possibilities of living life from the basis of "can I help?" not only when we are faced with someone who is clearly in need, but in any encounter with another. I believe most of us are more likely to be aware of the need for help when we are faced with someone in crisis. Most of the time, however, stewardship is not about giving in big, dramatic ways. More often, the need is much simpler. Sometimes, the need is so simple that we can easily fail to notice. An important part of stewardship, then, is to open our eyes, and our hearts, and become aware.

When I come home at the end of the day, Val is often engrossed in at least six tasks at once as she prepares supper and gives attention to our daughters. As some of you will have experienced, this is actually not the best time for me to ask "can I help?" As soon as I ask, of course, I have simply added a seventh task to her list: managing and directing me. What works better is to look around for myself, figure out what needs doing, roll up my sleeves, and get involved. This is very easy not to do. But the rewards of acting on my values—family, home, mutual support, love—are enormous and profound.

Ian West is a former administrator in both the hospitality industry, and in more recent years, in a long-term care facility for seniors in Calgary, Alberta. Ian is a stewardship leader, who holds in trust the facility that has been placed in his hands. He holds himself accountable for the well-being of the community—the staff, the residents, and the families of the residents in which he has been entrusted—by operating in service, rather than in control.[1] After a tour of his facility, in which I saw enormous compassion and commitment to *serve* those that he led, to honor those with whom he was entrusted, to support his staff so they might serve their residents from overflow rather than emptiness, we sat and reflected together in Ian's office about leadership and life.

"How would you describe your management philosophy?" I asked him.

He reflected momentarily and then drew my attention to a piece of art on a shelf beside his desk. Placed on the left-hand side of a slab of wood is a block of marble. On the right hand side Pu-tai, the laughing Taoist monk. Separating (or joining them) in the center is a clock, representing time. This is a visual reminder to Ian that his task, through time, is to intentionally chip away at the ignorance that conceals the genius inside each of his people within his steward, which, when revealed, shows a light-hearted, perfected being.

"It is important," he went on to say, "that the word 'remember' is used, as it is my contention that we are born with full knowledge and our task is to 'chip away' at our ignorance or forgetfulness. The 'perfect being' is contained in the marble waiting for the ignorance to be chipped away to reveal 'what god had put inside.' There is enormous dormant potential inside all of us."

[1] For a thorough exploration of Stewardship in the context of leadership, I refer to Peter Block's book, *Stewardship: Choosing Service Over Self-Interest*, Barett-Koehler Publishers, San Francisco, 1993.

To describe further the effect that well-intentioned management programs have had on this natural state of being, Ian drew another parallel between religion and spirituality. "Religion is *paint by numbers*; spirituality is the *masterpiece*. Religion is a prescription given for an ailing soul; spirituality is the spontaneous flow that prevents the ailment. The first is the response to sickness; the second, the presence of health. So many of our flavour-of-the-month management programs and gimmicks have offered a 'religious' approach. They offer paint-by-number, step-by-step quick fixes and heavy-handed solutions. They often begin from the premise that we do not 'know instinctively' the right way, so we have to learn."

"Leadership," Ian continued, "is a return to this natural state of *ease*. It is about knowing through remembering that order springs *naturally* from chaos, and that by encouraging the best climate, this order can be co-created more powerfully. Steward leadership is not about intercepting the chaos, as this only results in it ricocheting off into another 'unproductive' direction. Stewardship in organizations is a function of reflective thought and conscious action, which is more than skills and training. Unless issues of meaning, destiny, and greatness are nurtured and encouraged, we can't make a clear decision of what we will do today, much less build long-term strategy for an organization."

We have all experienced, and we have all been, people who help and people who hinder; people who lift and people who lean; people who contribute and people who consume. To give encouragement, offer support, show interest, and awaken hope in others is its own reward and returns to the giver many times over. Such gestures are noble and beautiful; they make the world a kinder, gentler place for all of us. Stewardship, the compassionate heart, is an integral part of a meaningful life. May we carry the lesson of the seas, and remember: to give is to live!

Act and Reflect:

Conduct a stewardship experiment tomorrow. Choose to be of service to the people you meet. Ask at least five people, "Can I help?" or better yet, just spot an opportunity and give what you can. Offer service to people you know, and to people you don't know. Be aware of what the people around you need to make their lives easier, and act accordingly!

At the end of the day, think and write about how the way of the compassionate heart changed your day. Stewardship is a conscious choice with great rewards.

Leg-up People

I rejoice in life for its own sake. Life is no brief candle to me. It is a sort of splendid torch, which I have got a hold of for the moment. And I want to make it burn as brightly as possible before handing it on to future generations.

—George Bernard Shaw

I was twelve years old when I saved up enough money to buy my first horse. Actually, Dad paid half, but for fifty dollars I got myself a retired pack horse named Caesar. All seventeen-hands and a six-inch protruding backbone was mine! I didn't have enough money for a saddle, so that first summer I learned to ride bareback. My grandpa used to say it was the only way to learn. I had a piece of baler twine for a bit and some old leather straps for reins. That's all I needed to have the time of my life, as long as I could get on, and stay on, that big old horse.

Enter Norris. Norris lived in an old dirt-floored log cabin down the road. He didn't have a possession to his name, except for an old bicycle and a couple of horses. He worked for my parents off and on as a hired hand for years, fixing fences, gardening, doing carpentry, building a barn. Norris was my hero when I was twelve. It was Norris who taught me how to hang onto a horse with my knees, and how to become one with that horse while I was riding on its back. It was Norris who taught me how a short, awkward twelve-year-old gets onto a seventeen-hand pack horse. At first, Norris got me to climb up on his leg and then jump from his knee onto the old gelding. Gradually, I was able to strengthen my arms enough that I could develop a technique for climbing onto the horse by myself.

Thinking back on that summer, I realized that Norris was my "leg-up person." (Thanks to Sid Simon for this term.) Norris was one of those people who comes along in your life and gives you an abundance of support, encouragement, and validation. For him, this was no great challenge. He simply showed up and cared.

To be a leg-up person for someone is to offer a special, invaluable kind of stewardship. Kids, especially, need a leg-up person in their lives. It does, as the saying goes, take a village to raise a child. Part of parenting is being a leg-up person, although we are more apt to spot the heroic qualities in our parents a few decades later than when we're growing up. Teaching responsibility and setting boundaries can make it tough to be seen as the hero. A leg-up person could be an aunt or uncle, a teacher or neighbor, a grandparent or just someone who cares; kids can never have too many of those.

Everywhere I go these days, I ask people who their heroes are. If you ask most kids, they'll often talk about people they've never met. Kids today are likely to have more celebrities as heroes than leg-up people they are connected to in a significant way. However, once in a while, when I ask kids and parents about heroes, I hear a story that touches my heart...

When I talked with the parents of eight-year-old Kyle Chrisman, ranchers from Big Piney, Wyoming, they said their son's hero was Brian Espenscheid. When I asked who Brian Espenscheid was, they told me, "Brian Espenscheid just graduated from the University of Wyoming and is a national caliber team roper. He grew up down the road from us and has always taken time for our boys. This summer, he taught Kyle, our eight-year-old, how to rope. And wouldn't you know it, for Halloween this year, Kyle would have nothing else but to dress up as Brian Espenscheid!"

In every community, and in every family, there is a Brian Espenscheid: someone who is willing to be a hero in a quiet way, someone who is there, someone who is willing to put his or her leg up and say "hop on." Our world needs this quality of character a great deal.

On the flip side, we might think about who were the leg-up people in our lives, and how can we best thank them. When I conduct workshops, I challenge the participants to write a letter or make a phone call of gratitude to one of their leg-up people (parents are often the ones who come to mind). I get to hear some great stories this way. Fathers, when they get a call and for the first time hear the words, "Dad, I admire you for being such a good father, and I love you," have been known to respond, "Have you been drinking?" or "Just a minute, I'll get your mother."

I'll never forget the workshop where a woman was called away by a family emergency at noon on the last day. Her dad was on his deathbed after suffering a sudden coronary attack; he passed away a few hours later. This woman's gratitude letter had been to her father. The miracle was, she had the opportunity to sit by his bed and read it to him before he died.

I wrote my own gratitude letter to my own dad, five years after he died. For the first time in my life, I thanked him for the times he took me fishing down the Blindman River near our home. We caught a lot of pike, and we lost a lot more, but I didn't notice until years later that Dad never fished on those outings. He paddled the canoe and untangled the line for an excited kid. So I took that letter to Dad's grave and I read it to him. In some way, that day, he spoke to me. He reminded me, as of course he would, that the most important thing was to go out and do the same for somebody else.

It would be remiss of me to write a chapter about leg-up people and not mention my courageous, compassionate, and wise mother, Joyce. Psychotherapist, social worker, philosopher, teacher, healer, and mentor, Joyce taught me, through the strength of her own life, that a fulfilling life is one that chooses principles over mere pleasure, contribution over self-centeredness, and authenticity over the desire for approval from the world. My mother recognized my gift and she nourished an upbringing that respected and supported the development of my unique talents. I recall vividly a conversation I had with her, shortly before her death in 1999, in which she spoke openly to me, of her love for the mystery, the wonder, and the miracle of life. "What makes us think we should ever have been born into this world? Every day is truly a miracle!"

"The word mystery means something secret, as if we see it with closed eyes. When we close our eyes we draw on a deeper kind of sight. We see at a deeper level. We see something we have not seen before. We learn to trust that a new creative expression will come to us from within. It flows out of inner vision. As we go down into the darkness of the feminine soul we discover a darkness that offers unlimited possibility. We discover a faith in our own 'being' that is unnamed, undefined, unmanifested."

Joyce then went on to share an experience of discovering a cave on a visit she had made to Ireland, some years before. "As I descended into its darkness, the sacred walked with me. A stillness, a holiness consumed the experience. Faint lights guided our path, but at one point, as we gathered in a circle, the guides extinguished the lights. We were in complete darkness. Only faith held me in those few moments. I had never been in such dark, dark, darkness. I surrendered into my faith and settled into the obscurity. I was held by it. I let my surrender have full range. A new energy with an overwhelming feeling of awe embraced me! I experienced the untold beauty of darkness. I felt I was in the womb of the earth and I stepped into unlimited possibilities for new creations. It was one of the creative peaks of my lifetime."

Such was the spirit of my mother. In tribute to her, I pass along to you a list below of some of the teachings, values, and perceptions related to simple living that I inherited from my mother, sometimes in her words, but mostly through the courageous life she lived.

- Change is. In all change is chaos, and in all chaos new order.
- Natural law is moving us from simple to complex as it is continually changing. To live simply in the ever-increasing complexity, it will become increasingly vital to sustain our own center.
- There is no security, except in our trust and our faith. There is only change. What holds us back is our fears and our resistance.
- Stand tall. Don't let anyone step on your spirit.
- As necessary as change is, if we are to move to a new order, not all change is good. We must never stop asking ourselves, in the midst of change, "What are our values that we must keep alive to align with the culture we want?" We must continually bring into light the values we hold dear.

- Problems can never be solved if we are in denial. First we must face our problems in order to correct them.
- Honor the feminine, both within yourself and within the world. Women in society are often the guardians of our deepest, most important values, so we must make our voices heard in the culture's arena.
- Money is not all that counts, and values must never go out of style.
- Never step away from speaking your truth. Even though the truth may not comfort you, it will liberate you.
- To live a full life, we must travel on four rivers: (a) the river of *inspiration*. I am still alive if I can be expanded and roused; (b) the river of *challenge*. I am still alive if I can be challenged to stretch, to move beyond the safe boundaries of the familiar; (c) the river of *surprise*. I am still alive if I can be delighted by the unexpected; and (d) the river of *love*. I am still alive if my heart is open, if I am being touched and moved by life.
- "Until you can take full responsibility for your life, you will not be fully alive," she would often say. Joyce gave me this definition of maturity: (a) the ability to do a job without being supervised; (b) the ability to finish a job once it is started; (c) the ability to carry money without spending it; and (d) the ability to be able to bear an injustice without wanting to get even.
- Joyce defined spirituality as walking the mystical path with practical feet. Spirituality is not about

going off into the mountains to meditate; rather it is seeing the sacred in every aspect of our lives in a way that continually feeds our souls and serves the world through our own deeper presence. She would often describe her daily experiences as spiritual: rocking a baby, watching a magnificent sunrise, experiencing a full moon on a winter night, breathing with the rise and fall of the ocean tide, comforting a hurt child, allowing someone to cry in her arms, watching a wolf lope across the bald prairie (oh, how Joyce loved the prairie and the ocean). These are what Joyce would describe as spiritual experiences, allowing ourselves to be inducted into the divine of life and know that there are forces greater than ourselves always available to us. "To me," she used to say, "spirituality is believing that we are each a unique manifestation of life with a unique destiny and we each have the responsibility of making choices that contribute to life. Each of us is a gift from and to the universe."

• People will have to learn to say what they fear to say, in places that matter, in order to sustain their lives.

Joyce did say what needed to be said in places that mattered, in many areas of society but none more important than with her children and grandchildren. On my forty-third birthday, the last before her passing, she gave me a book entitled, *The Moral Compass: Stories for a Life's Journey*.[1] Within the cover, she inscribed: "Dearest David, May these stories assist you

[1] William J. Bennett (editor) *The Moral Compass: Stories for a Life's Journey*, Simon & Schuster, Toronto, 1995.

in your desire to teach your girls the importance of connecting with the sacred of life... Much love to all of you on your journey, Mom."

Joyce honored those she loved. She had the gift to teach and heal, and anyone who knew her will be a witness to the manifestation of her gifts. She was a leg up to me by the life she lived, by her deep respect for me, by her wisdom and the mentoring she provided me, and with her patience and inner strength when I moved out from her shadow.

Simple living really is about the art of giving and receiving with a generous heart in our own unique way. So to all the leg-up people: the Norrises and the Brian Espenscheids, the fathers and the mothers, the teachers, the grandparents and the neighbors who have had a subtle and profound influence on so many others, thank you. I hope we can return the favor.

Act:

This is a two-part exercise: first, to say thanks to someone who offered a leg up to you, and second, to offer a leg up to someone else (which is, of course, a way of saying thanks for what you received by passing it on).

Make a list of all those who have been leg-up people in your life. This might include people who helped you as a child or as an adult, it might include family and community members, it might include people who are alive and those who have passed away.

Select one person on your list, and decide on an action you can take to say thank you. You may make a phone call from the heart, write a letter to read at a grave, give a donation or an offering in recognition, whatever is meaningful to you. The important thing is to find the courage to somehow communicate all the feelings you hold in your compassionate heart. You may find this feels so good that you keep working down the list!

There is someone in your community who could use a leg up from you right now. Look around, take your gifts, and share!

I Am Never Alone

God is the silent partner in all great enterprises.

— Abraham Lincoln

Every culture talks about God. Many names have been attached to the sacred aspect of life. The paradox for me is that, on the one hand, the search for a life of connection to the divine seems so complex, such a mystery. On the other hand, the journey can be so simple, if we are attentive and appreciate the divinity in each moment.

It's in the simple moments that I experience a life force beyond myself. I watch with great wonder as my children learn to walk, falls and all; I reflect on what inspires a child to talk. As I slow down and notice everyday miracles, I am overcome with a sense of awe in the simple but profound.

I was raised in a fundamentalist religion. As a youth, in the security of my religious doctrine, my

understanding of a higher power was limited. I just followed the rules. As I matured, I left my initial belief in
God behind. I took my spiritual search on a secular
journey through a series of personal development experiences, thinking enlightenment could be found "out
there" somewhere: in a book, a workshop, or a teacher.
As vital as these experiences were to my growth, however, they did not provide the sustained fulfillment I
was looking for. I eventually returned to my quest for
God, bringing new eyes to an old foundation.

In my struggle to survive the many crises since, I
began a relationship with a God different from the judg-
mental God I had learned of in church. For me, the path
to God lies within. It is not the dogmatic, fundamentalist, rigid approach to spirituality I interpreted as a child.
I have begun to experience God as a loving, down-to-
earth, personal God; a higher power that cradles,
supports, and carries me on life's journey; a God of
knowing that I am never alone. Connecting with this
sacred strength has enriched my life tremendously. Like
a friend, the God of my understanding has become
someone to talk to and lean on in all situations, through
quiet, still, solitary moments, and through prayer.

Looking back, the years I spent without a personal
relationship to God were spent in a fog, traveling in cir-
cles but never admitting I was lost. I kept myself so
busy, trying to control events and achieve success, that
from the outside I appeared to be in good shape. On the
inside, however, I wasn't experiencing all of life. Often

my accomplishments were ways to compensate for the truth that I was less than fully alive. My achievements became my drugs; my successes became the walls that held back fear. I reached a point in my life where these outer achievements and accomplishments, in and of themselves, became hollow, almost superficial. There grew an inner yearning for something more substantive, more lasting, more true.

Ultimately, choosing to trust in a higher power illuminates the sacredness in everyday life and lifts the veil. Choosing to trust in a power that transcends all human understanding opens the door for my life to change. I realize that I can get stuck hiding behind my fears. When I accept that there is a power greater than myself and surrender to that power, life improves. Surrender is ultimately about renunciation. It takes both courage and clarity to surrender: courage to renounce my will and attachment to that which is temporal, and clarity to seek a firm spiritual foundation to which I can submit.

Once a terrified man was suspended from a cliff two thousand feet above a valley floor. He strained his neck to look up to the top of the cliff and yelled, "Is there anyone up there who can help me?"

A deep, booming voice from above replied, "I'll help you. I'm God. Just relax and let go."

The now even more terrified man struggled to hang on as he looked down at the jagged stones in the valley below. Then he looked up and yelled in his loudest voice, "Is there anybody else up there who can help me?"

When I exchange fear for faith, I start to relax that stressed-out, cliff-edge grip I have on situations. Clarity enters my life. The process is like free fall; it's virtually effortless on a personal level. I have seen that the most powerful things in life occur when we don't try to work at them, control them, or will them into existence. All we do is surrender. This journey of surrender is not about ceasing to care; rather it is simply ceasing to control, to try and make it my way. There is a deep sense of inner peace that comes from this level of trust in God, a peace that truly surpasses all understanding, that transcends all outer success or failure. This peace transcends even my emotions; it can be present whether I am feeling "happy" or "sad."

I'm growing in this personal, spiritual connection with God, and I'm invigorated to find I can turn my life over to this power. I have spoken to many people who have begun to seek this connection to a higher power, through the contemplative journey that begins with slowing down and reaching for the divine power beyond our conscious understanding. The God of my experience is a constant companion, a powerful support, a friend. God's presence is a force that surpasses everyday fluctuations in self-worth, security, identity, and achievement. Gradually, I have been able to let go of traditional dependencies and surrender through a process of awareness, discovery, prayer, faith, and acceptance of life on life's terms.

In my daily search for a meaningful relationship with God, I have come to understand that I am never alone. A higher power helps me trust that spring will return when I'm surrounded by the depths of winter. It instills in me a sense of serenity, gratitude, and reverence for life. I live my life as a quest to explore my personal connection with the bounty of God. That's what spirituality means to me.

Reflect:

Take some time to reflect on the spiritual aspect of your life. Contemplate the statement by Teilhard de Chardin, that reflects my conviction that we are more than things, more than our physical existence. "We are not human beings having a spiritual experience. We are, rather, spiritual beings having a human experience."

four
SIMPLE LIVING

Stand firmly,
Sit serenely,
Mutter profoundly,
Sing outrageously,
And dance all the way to your death!

—James Broughten

Breakfast Friends

A friend is a person with whom I may be sincere.
Before a friend, I may think aloud.

—Ralph Waldo Emerson

For me, there are essentially two kinds of friends: lunch friends and breakfast friends. Lunch friends are people I spend an hour with. We have a chat or take care of business and then head back to work. Breakfast friends I can meet at nine in the morning and there's a good chance we'll still be talking at noon. Time seems to stand still with breakfast friends; they are the rare people with whom we can reveal our souls.

Far too often we allow ourselves to talk about the wrong things in life. So many of us are silent about what matters most, the deepest part of ourselves. We talk about cars and sports, hair, appearances, and clothes as we remain silent about our dreams, our hopes, and our values. We are mute about our deepest concerns, passions, and fears. Breakfast friends help us begin to change this.

Consider the following story a friend once told me of three such breakfast friends...

After graduating from university, Louise, Marion, and Claire left their parents behind and moved to the big city in search of careers in theater. Life was exciting but not without hardship. Their first Christmas money was scarce. The young women decided to get together over coffee one Sunday morning and make gifts to mail home to their families. As the morning stretched into a full day, and the Sundays stretched into weeks, the women crocheted, sewed, and knitted their friendship together.

When Christmas day arrived, hand-made parcels safely mailed, the women shared a special dinner. And they wept tears over the first Christmas spent without their families. In the New Year, they decided to continue meeting every Sunday morning over coffee. Because they were single and shared a sense of humor, they decided to call themselves The Spinster's Society. They laughed, cried, and supported each other every week for five years. Then as their lives changed shape, they moved on and went their separate ways.

Today, one is a manager in the oil industry, one is an entrepreneur, and one runs a theater company. They call and write, and when they all meet in the same city over coffee, it feels like no time has passed at all since that first meager Christmas. That's the way it is with breakfast friends.

I feel blessed in my life by my breakfast friends. Some are confidants to whom I open up my life, while others are mentors, who guide and give me renewed perspective on life. Often breakfast friends come into my life at a timely moment when their wisdom, their compassion, and their presence is mutually needed. Then we move on, both better people because of the time we spent together. Some breakfast friends are lifers and remain with us for all time.

I have, indeed, been blessed by Walter who has been in my life as long as he hasn't. Walter reaffirms and expands in me what my father first taught me about the nurturing power of love. He radiates compassion, acceptance, and life at its most essential core. Walter taught business classes in a college, until the day he chose to leave that career in order to experience the opportunities and responsibilities of being a full-time household executive and stay-at-home father. His life is a potent example of genuine connection, with himself, with others, and with the great force beyond.

Years ago Walter introduced me to the world of poetry—to Rumi, William Yeats, Walt Whitman, Robert Bly, Jane Kenyon, Bob Dylan, Mary Oliver, William Blake, and T.S. Eliot, to name a few. For a time we would take a chapter every month from Bill Moyer's *The Language of Life: A Festival of Poets*,[1] then meet and discuss it. For my forty-first birthday Walter bought me Czeslaw Milosz's *The Book of Luminous Things: An International Anthology of Poetry*. On the inside cover I

[1] Bill Moyer, *The Language of Life: A Festival of Poets*, Doubleday, New York, 1995.

found inscribed, "To David, a rare and precious breakfast friend! ...On your 41st ...I wish you much joy,
excellent health, good fortune, and a few of those rare
moments of 'beyond eternity' in the coming year... 'To
sail is necessary; to live is not.' (Plutarch) I admire and
love you.—Walter."
We live three hours apart, and have a favorite truck
stop where we meet for breakfast. Whenever we connect he brings me back to the source of life with
a reminder that life is more of an improvisation than a
strategic plan. On Walter's fiftieth birthday we sat and
read, together, a poem by William Butler Yeats, entitled, "Vacillation."[2]

> *My fiftieth year had come and gone,*
> *I sat, a solitary man,*
> *In a crowded London shop,*
> *An open book and empty cup*
> *On the marble table-top.*
> *While on the shop and street I gazed*
> *My body of a sudden blazed;*
> *And twenty minutes more or less*
> *It seemed, so great my happiness,*
> *That I was blessed and could bless.*

I have, indeed, been blessed by Walter's presence
over the years. He has mentored me through losses,
depressions, the early years of my marriage and the
raising of my young daughters. I, too, have been a support to him, an intimate witness to the entire spectrum

137

---

[2] Robert Bly, James Hillman, and Michael Meade (editors) *The Rag and Bone Shop of the Heart: Poems for Men*, HarperPerennial, New York: 1992, p. 507.

of the expression of his spirit—both the light and darker sides of his nature. He recently lost his brother and articulately described the experience, "Being with him during his final days on earth is akin to the brevity of life itself. For in those days of grieving, like the days of living, both are unbearable and beautiful."

I cannot speak of breakfast friends without sharing my gratitude for being blessed by my life-long partner, Valerie. Scott Peck once compared a good marriage to a base camp on the mountains you climb in life. It is that place of sanctuary, shelter, and renewal, where provisions are kept and where spirits and bodies are replenished, so you can turn and face each peak with revitalized strength. Successful mountaineers know that they must spend at least as much time, if not more, tending to their base camp as they actually do climbing mountains, for their survival depends upon their ensuring that their base camp is sturdily constructed and well stocked.

No truer metaphor could describe the way I feel about my marriage to Val. Val came to me as a gift many years ago and has been there every step of the journey. I would not be where I am today, either personally or professionally, if it were not for the love, the tenderness, and the deep respect we share for each other. Like a full moon on a dark winter night, Val reflects back to me the light needed to take me along many of the dark paths of life. Often in her desire to connect, I have been preoccupied. My obsession with being competent and successful has taken much energy away from her. Yet her compassionate heart remains open.

In the beginning of our relationship, Val was my rock, a stabilizing force in my life. Through her acceptance, combined with self-respect and her ability to set clear limits, I am learning to be stronger, to let go of self-centeredness, to be a giving partner in this life-long commitment. Like every long-term relationship, it has not been without both deep fulfillment and pain. It is with this life-long breakfast friend that I have opened up completely, expressing my dreams, my passions, and my deepest fears. Within the challenges and the immense joy we experience together comes the four corners of the life we are building together: respect, honesty, compassion, and hard work. Indeed, we are learning together how to create an intimate, equal, and enduring relationship.

We all need heartfelt friendships, but they don't always come easily. Over the past several years I have been investing daily in a spiritual community. It takes vulnerability, respect, tolerance, patience, and, above all, *time*, to build a community of breakfast friends, even if that community is one other person. Though nourishing breakfast friends is a challenge for most of us, men in particular in our society struggle to cultivate a close personal connection with one other person. We call it a successful male bond when we hug each other with ten layers of hockey equipment between us. If we desire a simple life, we need to be intentional about our

139

desire for more substantive, meaningful, open, trusting relationships in our lives.

Breakfast friends sustain and support you through both the good times and the bad, through the despair and through the dreams, through the darkness and the light. Breakfast friends care more about your spirit than they care about your ego. They, over time, will become truth-tellers, unencumbered by their need for your approval. They offer—and receive—that precious gift of both honesty and acceptance. Their importance in developing simplicity in life is something my words can never fully express; it is just something I know from the deepest part of my soul. Trying to get through life without a breakfast friend is like trying to survive a Canadian winter without a coat.

Reflect:

Draw a simple diagram of your network of friends and acquaintances. Place yourself in the center. Place your breakfast friends in close to you and your lunch friends further away. Identify the gifts you receive in each of these relationships. Circle the names of the people you would like to see more.

Act:

Pick up the phone and call a friend you haven't seen for a while—one who nurtures within you a sense of competence and possibility. Invite him or her out for breakfast. Talk about your dreams together. Learn to support each other as you begin to stretch your human boundaries by taking risks and failing. Start small. It only takes one other person to begin a breakfast friend relationship.

If, for whatever reason, your network of friends is too thin, make a list of all the people that are possible sources of new friends in your life (relatives, colleagues, church or club members, friends-of-friends, and so on). What action can you take to cultivate at least one breakfast friend in your life?

There Are No Bad Days,
Only Bad Thoughts

There is no such thing as bad weather; there is only bad clothing.

—Hugh and Dick Bradley, Ranchers,
   330 kilometers north of Whitehorse, Yukon

I was aboard an airplane one day, flying home, when I met a remarkable woman. After being served my meal, I was ready to start complaining to the person beside me about how tired I was of airline food, how cramped the seats on the airplane were, how long the delay before take-off had been. Before I could speak, my seat companion turned to me and commented on the helpful service she had received on the plane, how fortunate we were to be able to enjoy such a fine meal, and how happy she was to be flying to visit her grandchildren.

I asked her where she found her optimism. "I am from Sarajevo," she replied. "I have seen my friends and many of my family shot. Then I joined my family here. Since I came to this country, every day is a good day for me." She talked about her homeland, and about flying on an airplane where you would never get a meal, the plane is full of flies and dirt, and those things don't matter as much as just being able to get off the ground without being hit by mortar and bullets.

She explained one of the reasons the world seems to be falling apart is because we don't see the good in the world any more. She told me the good that came out of the war for her was that she appreciates every waking moment of her life, and that she deeply cherishes the peace that allows her to visit her daughter and her grandchildren. She said, "I have learned that there really are no bad days. There are only bad thoughts."

When I got off the plane, I waited more than the usual three minutes for the bus that was to take me to my parked truck. The driver was fifteen minutes late, and as I started to feel impatient, I remembered the words of that wise woman on the plane: "There are no bad days. There are only bad thoughts." I knew full well that there were more important things to get concerned about than waiting a few minutes. I felt grateful that I didn't have to walk the fifty kilometers to my house, and that I had a safe home to go to and a family who loves me.

When the bus arrived, I smiled at the young driver. He looked tired. "Thanks for your patience," he said. "It's been a long day."

When the bus driver dropped me off at my truck, I noticed two vehicle owners arguing. Curiosity got the best of me, and I sat with my window down listening to their heated discussion. One of the men had opened his door and inadvertently chipped the side panel on the other man's car. "I am going to sue you for the money it will take to replace that panel!" yelled the chipped-car driver. Admittedly, I was not privy to all that had happened prior to this exchange, but again I remembered my conversation with the woman on the plane and thought about how insignificant situations can upset us to the point of insanity. There are no bad days, only bad thoughts.

On my way home, I reflected on the situations I get upset about that really don't matter in life's big picture: getting cut off on the freeway, spending an extra five minutes in a check-out line, spilling lunch on my shirt, anything that doesn't work right on the first try. A lot of trivial matters consume my energy. It's all too easy to define our days as either good or bad based on the number and severity of our petty annoyances.

The innocence of children is often a great mirror to teach us about attitude...

A mother drove through rush hour traffic with her five-year-old son at her side. The young boy looked around inquisitively, hands on the dashboard, seat belt taut. "Mom," he asked, "Where are all the jerks and idiots?"

"What?" she responded. "Jason, where did you learn that kind of language?" There was no reply.

They drove on in silence while the mother puzzled about what her son was talking about. Then suddenly she got it. "Oh," she said. "They only come out when your Dad drives!"

Everything we experience is filtered through the lens of our perception. We don't see the world as it is; rather, we see the world as we are. So much of how we experience our lives has far more to do with our perception of our lives than with outside circumstances, or the behavior of others. Inner peace is fostered by the inner journey to connection, and by patience, kindness, and the knowledge that everyday attitude is a choice. Much of the time it is true: there really are no bad days, there are only bad thoughts.

When I arrived home at the end of my journey that day, Val met me at the door and said, "Welcome home. You must have had a tough week."

I kissed her and said, "No, it's been a great week. Thanks for caring. How can I help?"

Reflect:

Can you go for one whole day without expecting anything from anyone? This will likely be harder than it sounds. Apply the "no expectations" attitude to family members, office associates, clerks in stores, drivers on the road, and everyone you do any kind of business with for one day. Don't expect fast service, don't expect people to get out of your way, don't expect dinner to be ready, don't expect anything! Try this just for one day, and notice what happens!

What does this experience teach you about how many expectations you carry into each day? Might your attitude towards life be proportional to your level of expectation?

The Little Things

We ourselves feel that what we are doing is just a drop in the ocean. But if that drop was not in the ocean, I think the ocean would be less because of that small drop. I do not agree with the bigger way of doing things. To us what matters is the individual.

—Mother Teresa

Once at a business conference I talked briefly about my own family business, and the joys and challenges of working with the ones you love. Shortly after my return home, Val received a gift in the mail. It was a delicate gold ornamental fish accompanied by a brief note.

Dear Val,

Thank you for enabling your husband to speak at the conference we attended. It can't be easy for you with David traveling so much, but his information certainly blessed us.

He spoke so highly of you. You must be very special. Thanks again!

Gail.

Val's life brightened on the day that note arrived. She phoned me and her excitement was infectious; I grabbed a cab and gave the driver a substantial tip. He turned to me and said, "Thank you. You are very kind. I have three children, and shoes these days are very expensive." I smiled and thought how Gail's generosity had multiplied.

I didn't meet Gail in person until years later, but her act of kindness made an enormous impact on my wife and our family. After the small gift arrived, we talked about the importance of little things and what a difference a small, spontaneous act of kindness can make. Gail, wherever you are today, thank you for touching a life, for making a difference to a family and perhaps even to the world. In relationships, as perhaps in life, it is truly the little things that are the big things.

Since that time, I have often wondered if our hectic work environments and communities would change if we all performed one small act of kindness for another person every day. When I remember Gail's unsolicited kindness, I also think of Jo, a nurse who came to my rescue during one of the most humiliating and, in retrospect, humorous experiences of my life...

Val and I had tried for two years to conceive a child. Even though we were having great fun trying, eventually we decided to utilize the services of an infertility clinic. At the clinic, we went through a series of humbling tests to assess my sperm count and evaluate Val's ovulation cycle. On one occasion, I (or at least my semen) was needed for a procedure. I arrived at the fertility clinic, only to discover that the sperm bank had been moved. Wandering through a clutch of patients in the waiting room, I approached the nurse and whispered, "Could you tell me where the sperm bank has moved?"

She peered at me over her glasses and then shouted down the corridor so every person in the waiting room could hear, "Where is the sperm clinic?"

A loud voice responded, "The sperm what?"

"The sperm clinic!" she virtually screamed.

"I don't know!"

I turned without saying a word and walked past all those staring, smiling faces out the door.

I went across the hall and asked another nurse the same question. She gave me a detailed description of the location. I thanked her and left, realizing halfway down the hall that I was so embarrassed, I hadn't heard a word she had said.

Now I was angry. I went to the information desk and asked the clerk there the same question. I got lost trying to follow his directions. Finally, I found a janitor. I never felt so grateful for the man who cleans the hospital. I asked him where the sperm hang out, and he mercifully gave me simple directions I could follow.

I finally found the sperm clinic, made my donation, and headed back to the infertility clinic, which also had been moved. I approached the front desk to request some information on the procedure. In the move, the infertility clinic had lost my file. They had no record of

149

me or my sperm! The clerk asked me what procedure I was here for. This was the third procedure we had been through, I was way past flustered, and so naturally I couldn't recall its name.

This clerk asked me to take a seat, explaining that all the nurses were busy but someone would be with me soon. Five minutes later a nurse stuck her head through the door of the crowded waiting room and yelled, "Where's the patient with the question about his sperm count?"

Much to my chagrin, I lost all control. I stormed up the aisle in a major huff, saying, "When you people can get your act together, give me a call and I'll come back!"

As I turned to go, another nurse slipped through the waiting room door and called to me. I immediately felt her compassionate heart. With one gesture of her hand, she signaled to me to step into her office.

"Hi, my name's Jo," she said. "What can I do to help you?"

I heard the kindness in her voice, and I sat down and cried before any words could come. Then I told her of the morning's frustrations and of our long struggle to conceive a child. In the end, she located my file and gave me some simple directions about the next step in the procedure.

Jo took five minutes out of her busy day to comfort a distressed soul. She probably didn't learn that in an interview class in university. It was not part of her job description, nor was it a complex skill that required years of practice or would have earned her a raise. She was just one individual who cared enough to put her professional face aside and show concern for a hurting soul. I left the infertility clinic that day feeling better than when I came in. Nine months after the procedure, Val gave birth to a wonderful, healthy, seven-pound baby girl.

I sent a thank-you note to Jo a few days after our meeting. I only met her once, but there is an interesting ending to this story. A colleague of Jo's was in a presentation I gave to the Calgary Health Region a few years ago. This colleague purchased a copy of one of my earlier editions of *Simple Living* and passed it on to Jo. A few days later, a heart-felt thank-you card was waiting in my mailbox for me from Jo, expressing her gratitude that I had been so thoughtful as to include her name in this book. What goes out into the world will truly come back to us. We need to notice and nurture the Jo's we meet every day, people who care enough about their jobs and other people to show some much needed love in our busy world.

Yes, one small act of kindness does make a difference.

Act:

For the next week, practice a new style of giving. Take a few minutes every day, and give a "little thing." You might give someone at the office a compliment, tip the paperboy for no reason at all, send a note of thanks to someone who is unlikely to expect it, or bring a friend some flowers. Make a note in your daytimer to do one "little thing" every day for the next seven. Keep track of what you do, and notice how you feel.

Then start to think about how you can integrate "little thing" thinking into your life. It's a great idea, for example, to keep some nice cards and stamps on hand, so that you can easily send a loving thought, or a funny one, to someone you know. Be creative! Be a generous giver of "little things!"

Finding Your Future in the Present

We do not remember days, we remember moments.

—Cesare Pavese

"We are clever people, efficient and high-powered, but in our zeal to get things done we are forgetting the simple art of living... Let us make a resolve that we will begin today to relax, and loiter, and potter around, and be lazy if we feel like it once in a while, and take time to meditate, and watch the sun go down behind the hill... Let us be good to ourselves." No truer statement could be said in response to the complexity of our post-modern era. What is surprising, however, is that this statement was not written in the twenty-first century. It was, instead, written by Nellie L. McClung, and taken from her book entitled *Be Good to Yourself*, copyright 1930!

These words are a good reminder that the lack of simplicity in our lives is not just a recent phenomenon. It would appear that we have been struggling with this idea of simplicity for quite sometime. My own struggle has led me to find four keys to simplicity: finding clarity, making room, being present, and adhering to a practice.

Finding Clarity

A rich industrialist from the North was horrified to find a Southern fisherman lying lazily beside his boat, smoking a pipe.

"Why aren't you fishing?" asked the industrialist.

"Because I have already caught enough fish for the day," replied the fisherman.

"Why don't you catch some more?"

"What would I do with then?"

"You could earn more money," responded the industrialist. "With that you could have a motor added to your boat to go into deeper waters and catch more fish. Then you would make more money to buy more nylon nets. These would bring you more fish and more money. Soon you would have enough money to own two boats...maybe even a fleet of boats. Then you would be rich like me."

"And what would I do then?" asked the fisherman.

"Then you could really enjoy life."

"What do you think I am doing right now?"

Parker Palmer once wrote, "Movements begin when people refuse to live divided lives." This Southern fisherman did not have simplicity in his life just because he was relaxing and having a "stress-free" life. This fisherman had simplicity in his life and was "stress-free" *because* he held the first key to simplicity—*clarity*. He was not divided. He knew what he wanted in his life and aligned his choices with what mattered most. His life reflected—either consciously or unconsciously—his core values. He did not succumb to the force of popularity, power, or prestige or approval from the world—all of which corrode simplicity—in order sustain his worth. Regardless of your judgment of this fisherman for the kind of life he was living, his clarity is undisputable.

In 1989, when I was closing down my psychotherapy practice as my seminar and speaking business was beginning to grow, I traveled over two hundred days. I was centered completely on my business, working appointments with my psychotherapy clients in between when I was home. I was talking about balance and connections, and meaning, while *experiencing* a life that was immensely out of balance and relationships that were suffering. My life was divided and therefore lacked simplicity.

Although this was a necessary stage in the development of my business and my life, over the following years I experienced a series of wake-up calls, pulling me back into balance. I was aloof and silent when I wasn't working, and isolated myself into a protective cocoon. I became sick every time I took a holiday. I missed important appointments with important people in my life and shrugged off the guilt with more work. I suffered ever-increasing mood swings, and covered up my anxiety and loneliness with more busyness. The unacknowledged frustrations began to turn to rage, which I released on both myself and those closest to me.

I would lie awake at night, replaying the phone calls, the presentations, and the conversations, worrying that I had everything in my inbox appropriately taken care of. As I look back on this very manic time in my life, I realize that I was not living my life, but rather my life was living me. I was not running my business; my business was running me. Indeed, I was clinging to work the way an addict clings to drugs. Work enabled me to escape from myself, and in the process, I was progressively losing touch with the vital life force and connections in my life that sustain me. I was spinning a web that was not only defining me, but was also concealing me. Just as in any addiction, the journey progressively took me to a point of despair and desperation over the ensuing years. I needed to start my journey home—a journey back to simple living.

During a holiday with Val, I took the time to reflect on my life and work, and actually began applying some of the exercises outlined in this book. As I slowed down, I realized that amidst all the success I was experiencing, I was not at peace with myself. Something was missing, and I knew that more of the same, more of the busy treadmill would not fill my inner void.

For the first time in my life, I began to take heed of some of my own advice. I had spent years giving people a formula for creating their future. It consisted first of defining a quality of life for yourself and with the important people in your life, and then deciding how much and what kind of production will be necessary to support the kind of quality of life you want. Sounded simple. It was time to put my "formula" to work.

The next five years became a process of practicing and refining a guide—a blueprint for a simple and meaningful life with myself, my family, and colleagues. During those years I learned much. My life remains an unfinished work of art. However, I have now begun to understand that there is a simple guide for finding balance in our complex world.

Most important is to gain clarity by answering three vital questions: (i) What matters most to me? (ii) What is the quality of life that I—and those closest to me—desire? and (iii) What is the level of production needed to sustain this quality of life? Simplicity finds its way into our lives when production (our work) becomes a tool or means for creating what we want in life, rather than an end in itself.

In 1967, Charles Hummel, who inspired Stephen Covey (author of *Seven Habits of Highly Effective People*), wrote a little book called *The Tyranny of the Urgent*. In that book, Hummel makes a vital distinction between "urgent" and "important." Urgency has to do with demands from others that intrude upon us and insist on our immediate attention. "Important" are those things that go beyond the pressing and are aligned with the overall direction and focus of one's life. When you begin to discern the difference between the "urgent" and the

157

"important" things in your life, you will find that the important things are, in fact, not "things" at all.

Hummel made a profound statement as he saw society moving into such a demanding time that we would soon become slaves to the tyranny of urgency. Writes Hummel, "The important task rarely *must* be done today, or even this week. The urgent task calls for *instant* action. The momentary appeal of these tasks seems irresistible and important, and they devour our energy. But in the light of time's perspective, their deceptive prominence fades. With the sense of loss we recall the vital task we pushed aside. We realize we have become slaves to the tyranny of the urgent."[1]

Being clear on your vision of an ideal quality of life and your core values gives you a compass or framework for decision-making. When you have clarity, and someone intrudes on an evening with your children by requesting you take a volunteer position on a board in your community, you can politely ask them to call back in twenty-four hours while you decide if this "urgent" request is, in fact, also important. You will find that saying no, a requirement for a simple life, will become easier as you get clear on what matters most. Out of the clarity will come a powerful "to-do" list, where the important things in your life will be scheduled in your day planner in advance. But most importantly, this kind of clarity will enable you to formulate a "don't-do list," a list of those things that may be expected of you but simply are not important. As you develop a strong "don't-do" list, a

[1] Charles E. Hummel, *The Tyranny of the Urgent*, Intervarsity Press, Downers Grove, Illinois, First edition, 1967; Rev. Ed. 1994.

courageous and respectful statement of what is the extent of your commitment, you will begin making room for what matters most, and simplicity will begin to emerge from within the smothering rubble of urgency.

Simplicity surfaces when there is congruence between your core values and your daily choices. A life without balance is one that either lacks clarity about what matters most, or lacks the courage of alignment. Fulfillment of my desire for simplicity—and subsequent meaning—grows from the choices I make each and every day: the choices to live honestly, with awareness, and in alignment with my deepest values. As I spend conscious effort reflecting upon my values, clarity emerges and evolves. I share with you my own personal values in the spirit of respect. My hope is that you will not follow the path of my values but rather that you stake out your own, and, with confidence, leave your own trail.

My first and most important value, and upon which all else is built, is my *faith*. Faith is a deep and sustaining reliance on a power greater than myself, to which I surrender daily. Faith is the source of my security, worth, stability, wisdom, and perspective. Anyone who has spent time at sea knows that to avoid seasickness, you must keep your eyes firmly on the horizon. Faith is my stable horizon in the waves of life. God, as I understand God in my own personal way, is the guiding force in my life, the partner in all my ventures. In my daily quiet time I find strength in prayer, in gratitude, and attending to this life force. My greatest

159

responsibility is to be a helper rather than a destroyer of the treasures in nature's storehouse, a partner in caring for the vineyard that has been given to me. I am, prepared to stand one day, before my maker, the creator of the universe, with no other plea than that I sought attentively for clarity of God's will in my life and the strength to carry that out, and that I tried to leave this world better than I found it.

My second value is a *strong character*. In 1944, in Marzobotto, a small town near Bologna in Italy, two thousand civilians were massacred by Nazi troops. The Nazis were retaliating for acts of sabotage committed by members of the Italian resistance. One young German soldier, however, refused to take part in the massacre and was shot. In my imagination, that man experienced true freedom, the freedom that comes from being a person of strong character. He put truth and justice above obedience to superiors and his desire to live at any cost.[2]

Inspired by the examples throughout history of men and women who refused personal advancement, wealth, and power because they wanted to live in accordance with their conscience, who chose principles over pleasure, my second core value is that I desire to be a person with strength of character.

Aristotle identifies what he termed "external goods," such as wealth, property, power, and reputation. Twenty-three centuries ago, he taught that the good life is not one of more consumption but consists of the flourishing of our deepest selves. Consumer goods are the elements

[2] Cited in Jean Vanier, *Becoming Human*, p.108.

that make up the popular vision of success—both then and now. To these, Aristotle contrasts elements of character, what he termed the "goods of the *soul*," including fortitude, temperance, justice, and wisdom.[3] We continue to make this distinction between the inner and the outer as we reflect on the matters of worldliness and the matters of virtue, both in our own lives and in the lives of the children we influence. What, after all, would you rather leave your children: a rich financial inheritance with no values and character, or values and character with no money? With values and strength of character, we can create wealth and much more.

Strong character is expressed in the virtues I want to be known for, both through the eyes of the world, and through the eyes of my soul when I look at myself in the mirror at the end of a day. Strong character calls me from being the best *in* the world to being the best *for* the world. While I continue to gain clarity about my values, they are essentially fixed, while virtues are those qualities I work on daily. They include such things as:

- *Humility*—I am dedicated to the search for truth, to the acceptance of life on life's terms, and to reliance on a God as my source of direction and strength.
- *Integrity*—I am honest in my dealing with all people, and by keeping promises to myself and others, I am aligned with my conscience and have self-respect.
- *Principled*—I attempt to make decisions and promises in my life based on what is right, rather

[3] Aristotle, *Politics*, trans. Ernest Barker, New York: Oxford University Press, 1961, p. 26, cited in *Graceful Simplicity: Toward a Philosophy and Politics of Simple Living*, by Jerome Segal, p. 5.

than on fleeting emotions or a need for acceptance or approval from others.

- *Maturity*—I claim full ownership of my life—without blame.
- *Prudence*—I seek the common sense to decide what I can do *without* and the ability to find joy in what is here.
- *Compassion*—I have a sincere desire to live life with an open heart and bring kindness and grace to my relationships.
- *Vulnerability*—I live life without pretence, bringing a quality of humanness to all areas of my life and work.
- *Contribution*—I have an ongoing commitment to overcome self-centeredness.
- *Gratitude*—I feel awe and reverence for the blessings that have been bestowed upon me.

Your character, which comes from aligning your choices with your virtues, forms the inner foundation that will sustain you. I think of one of my mentors in the area of strong character, Don Campbell, who ranches in Northern Saskatchewan. "You could lose it all—your animals, your land, even your entire ranch, but no one can take away your character without your consent. When your wealth is lost, something is lost; when your health is lost, a great deal is lost; when your character is lost, everything is lost."

Within my third value of *marriage and family*, my

first priority is my life-long partnership with Val so we can be more fully engaged with our children—together. We respect, support, and encourage each other and hope to grow old holding hands and hearts. I also put my best effort forward to ensure that I am the best possible father to my three daughters. By showing them that they are both lovable and capable, I envision them becoming interdependent, responsible, contributing adults from the solid foundation I am helping to build today. Making time for extended family is also vitally important to me. My value of marriage and family teaches me that love is not a noun; love is a verb. Love is not a feeling; love is an action. Love is spirituality in action. The words of one of my early mentors, David O. McKay, remain with me. "No other success can compensate for failure in the home"

My fourth value is *health*—I recognize that good health is a source of wealth in my life, and never to be taken for granted. Health means a strong and sustaining body to carry my soul. Genetics are a given, but I can influence my health, even if I can't control it. I want to sustain balanced habits of beneficial nutrition, rest, moderate, enjoyable aerobic exercise, along with some flexibility, and strength training on a weekly basis. In former years, as a competitive distance runner, I learned that if you don't give your body rest, it will not strengthen and will depreciate. Recently I began the practice of yoga and Pilates. I also enjoy regular massages to tune in to my body. My body is not just a vehicle; it is also a good barometer for what is going on in my life. When I am taking on too much of the world's problems, I first feel it in my shoulders. If I am I picking up too much fear or anxiety, it will surely register in my neck. The sooner and more attuned I am to my body, the more responsive I can be to guiding my life toward simplicity.

My fifth value is *stewardship*. Stewardship is the ongoing discovery and authentic expression of my gifts in a way that serves the world. I am a steward of the talents that I have been given for this short life journey, and I use them consciously in the service of others. My business—my work—is a tool to support and sustain my values, especially my commitment to being a steward of the gifts that have come my way. It is extremely fulfilling to build a profitable business, but the sustaining power of my work is the values and virtues that lie at the core of my business. As my friend, Ray Nelson, said, "It's easy to make a buck, but it is important to make a difference."

Stewardship also is a commitment to life-long learning. Although I read extensively (and have provided a reading list at the back of the book for those wanting to learn more about simple living), I learn best through conversations and actively seek out mentors and coaches in the key areas of my life. I solicit feedback from others wherever and whenever I can, and I seek to expand my self-awareness on a regular basis. You can't do it alone.

My sixth value is *community*. My commitment to community means surrounding myself with people who support me and hold me accountable for living out my deepest values and intentions; people who care deeply for my soul and are committed to walk with me along this journey. Community also means being encircled by a rich, diverse, and sustaining ecosystem, and a commitment to make choices that sustain our environment.

Having clarity about my core values—what I want in my life—gives me a beacon, a compass, and thus a foundation, in my life. I take time, in my annual inventory of my business and my life, to reflect upon these values, refine them, and make an assessment of how I did with them in the past year. My family and those closest to me know what my values are and I regularly solicit their input as to my progress. Each year I set goals in each of the six areas to give me some focus for the coming year. They are typed into the front of my day planner, and when I plan my week, I ensure that I pay attention to them at least weekly, if not daily.

When I live each day as an expression of my defining values, I stop looking outside myself for all the answers. I know a greater sense of peace and trust, and I experience a heightened awareness of what's going on within me and around me. I find comfort in simply being, rather than always doing. Instead of worrying about controlling the future, I live each day with the clarity of knowing what I stand for in the present. One of my favorite stories about self-discovery, the Eastern European tale of Susa inspired by Angles Arrien, speaks of the importance of knowing who I am...

At a time when his village was experiencing great suffering, Susa went to the top of a nearby mountain to seek a sign. Long ago, Susa had learned that the character of any nation is built on its people's concern for the poor, the elderly, the sick, and the young. So he knelt on the wind-blown peak, and prayed for the guidance he needed, well into the night.

At sunrise, he returned to the village terrified. The community gathered around him and asked, "Susa, why are you so afraid?"

Wide-eyed, Susa replied, "I now know what the angels will ask me on the last day."

The people were surprised that this wise man was worried about his last day. "Susa, you have lived such a model life," one of the elders said.

"And you have been of such support to your community," said a young widow.

"Oh," Susa replied, "they are not going to ask me why, like Moses, I didn't lead my people out of slavery into the promised land."

"What, then, are they going to ask you?" the people inquired.

Susa looked toward the mountain peak and replied, "They are going to ask me, 'Susa, why weren't you Susa?'"

I believe there are three stances we can adopt as we lift our eyes and face our lives as Susa did. The first is the victim stance; when we live from this perspective we make choices based on the belief that life is beyond our control. The second is the controller stance; living from this perspective means to make choices motivated by fear, and by the desperate need to control life's events so that nothing uninvited will happen. The third is the heroic stance. To live from the heroic stance is to welcome change, watch for guideposts and teachers, build deep connections, and express defining values every day. There is an elegant balance and simplicity in knowing who we are, and living accordingly. If we can focus on our values in the present, we will surely become the true self we seek in the future. Along the way, we will have much to celebrate, both in our achievements and in our connections.

The choice is ours, every single day. Everything each of us has done to this point in our lives has only been a beginning.

Making Room

In the Zen tradition of Buddhism there is a story of a smart and eager university professor who comes to an old Zen master for teachings. The Zen master offers him tea and upon the man's acceptance he pours the tea into the cup until it overflows. As the professor politely expresses his dismay at the overflowing cup, the Zen master keeps on pouring.

"A mind that is already full cannot take in anything new," the master explains. "Like this cup, you are full of opinions and preoccupations." In order to find happiness, he teaches his disciple, he must first empty his cup of old beliefs and attitudes.[4] In order to find

167

4 Paul Reps, *Zen Flesh, Zen Bones*, New York, Anchor Books, 1961, p. 5

simplicity, we must empty our own cup and make room for what matters most in our life.

As you prepare the way for a simpler life, you will need to create the space for something new to enter. And creating space for something new first requires a willingness to let go. We move toward simplicity by simply clearing away some of the clutter in our lives, those objects that gather in our living space and block the door for simplicity to enter.[5]

"Making room" requires the habit of asking ourselves, "What can I take out of my day today to make room for what matters most?" As you become increasingly clear about your core values, you may want to say no to a commitment in your community to make room for a loved one. You may want to say no to a lunch meeting in order to go for a walk. You might decide to start spending less money than you earn, making room for a financial cushion in your life. Nothing will annihilate simplicity more than economic pressures from overspending. Gradually, as you develop the daily habit of making room, simplicity will begin to emerge, for you will find yourself having made room to breathe, to live more fully, and to be present to the experience of life.

A friend told me of his visit with members of his Christian fellowship in communist China a few years ago. He was greeted at the base of the Great Wall with a warm handshake and the quiet but definite sign of the cross on the inner side of his palm.

"We are so concerned for you who live in North

[5] For a more detailed examination of making room for simplicity, see *Becoming Real: Journey to Authenticity*, by David Irvine, pp. 120–125.

America," his communist brother exclaimed. "Our sympathy here in China goes out to you."

My friend wondered why a person living amidst a communist regime could possibly feel sorry for a person who lived in the blessed continent of North America, so he asked, "Why would you be concerned for us?"

"Because you have *so much* that gets in the way between you and God. You have so many distractions..."

Whether your goal is to get closer to God or closer to a little simplicity in your life, *making room* will be a needed step.

Being Present

A Zen monk, when pursued by a ravenous tiger, climbed halfway down a cliff and hung by a branch above a ledge where he found an equally ferocious tiger. Growing next to the branch was a bush with a single strawberry, which the monk picked. He smelled the strawberry, felt the strawberry, ate the strawberry... and thought to himself, "How delicious!"

It has been said that the best present we can give to someone is the present of being fully present in the present. Of course, this gift of being present in the present begins with a gift to ourselves. As you become aware of the present, as you experience it, you change your relationship to time. The rush of the past and the worry of the future—those twin tigers—are cast aside. There is no stress in the present. In the present we find ultimate simplicity.

169

The best way to capture the present moment is to practice paying attention, or being mindful.[6] Mindfulness means being awake. "Only that day dawns to which we are awake," wrote Henry David Thoreau, who spent two years at Walden Pond, which, above all, was a personal experiment in mindfulness. He chose to put his life on hold in order to experience the wonder and simplicity of present moments. But you don't have to spend two years on Walden to practice mindfulness. It is enough to make a little time in your life for stillness, and for what we call "doing nothing." Simply noticing your breathing is a way of being present. Just *being*—without any judgment—with your loved ones, with the beauty that surrounds you, with yourself, and even with the frustrations and pressures in your life, are ways of staying present. Try asking yourself, at this moment, "Am I awake?" "Where is my mind right now?" "What am I feeling?" "What is happening to my body right now?"

Being present teaches us that beauty is always there if we are open enough to see it. Being present allows us to open to the magnificence just behind the thin curtain of the ordinary. In my counseling practice, I was privileged to be present to the raw vulnerabilities of people's inner lives, to experience the beauty and grace behind their pain. Witnessing my father's struggle with mental illness, and walking with him through some of his tumultuous breakdowns, I learned that just on the other side of unspeakable anguish and desolation lay a vast landscape of beauty that graced his life,

[6] For a thorough and practical guide to mindfulness, see Jon Katat-Zinn's book, *Wherever You Go There You Are: Mindfulness Meditation in Everyday Life.*

and the lives of those who were close to him, with immense wisdom, compassion, and creativity. I am convinced that none of these amazing qualities would have been present in his life if Harlie had not been present to his manic depressive illness.

While writing this chapter, I was sitting, preoccupied, during my seven-year-old daughter's gymnastics class. I had a sudden awareness—what I know now as a moment of grace—when, in the midst of her practice I caught myself writing about being present, while missing the present magnificence of young children doing cartwheels on a beam. My experience, at that moment, is beyond words. The ordinary, suddenly noticed, became the "awe-dinary." There is so much to celebrate in the world when we stop and simply pay attention to the miracle of life. Incredible things happen when we stop and are open to what surrounds us.

Living in the present—an essential habit of simple living—is the art of catching up with ourselves. It is about cultivating a more intimate awareness of the world, despite the losses and vulnerability involved with that intimacy. As we become more fully present in the world, we free ourselves from the pull of the world. By facing the vulnerabilities in my own life such as the loss of both my parents, the ending of relationships, spiritual bankruptcy, and depression, I am able to find some peace amidst the pain and the joy. I have less need to escape from reality, for it is being present in reality that brings peace—and eventually simplicity. "Eternity has nothing

171

SIMPLE LIVING

to do with the hereafter..." writes Joseph Campbell. "This is it ... If you don't get it here, you won't get it anywhere. The experience of eternity right here and now is the function of life. Heaven is not the place to have the experience; here's the place to have the experience."

Adhering to a Practice

So, once you are able to find and capture some simplicity in your life, how do you keep it? The key to maintaining simplicity in the midst of the complexity is establishing habits which, when practiced daily, will help keep you on track. Simple living, to be sustained, is not a theory; it is a practice, and this practice is fueled by a desire to grow. Without a desire to better ourselves, to continue to seek new consciousness in our lives, we will, in all likelihood, not be able to sustain simplicity. In order to keep our lives simple, we have to want more than simplicity. Simplicity necessitates a yearning to expand.

There are many contemplative practices available today, and regardless of the one you choose, the key is to find one that is right for you and stick to it.[7] A few elements that are common to most forms of sustained practices include: (a) *contemplation*, a daily routine of quiet time, a time for meditation, reflection, and prayer, (b) self-examination, observing daily what is happening—in your body, in your heart, in your mind, (c) a *community* of support, confidants that you can open up with daily, and who will hold you accountable for choosing a life that is in alignment with your core

172

[7] For a more in-depth process of finding a spiritual practice that is right for you, see the last chapter in my book, *Becoming Real: Journey to Authenticity.*

values, and (d) and a *commitment to service*, to move beyond self-centeredness.

The velocity of the world today, combined with the onslaught of email, voice mail, and other demands that surround us, seems antithetical to creating space for simplicity. In the midst of the pressure, we are all attempting to create lives and workplaces that are more adaptive, flexible, and capable of adjusting to a dynamic world. To accomplish this daunting task, we must adhere to a daily practice that provides us with the space and time to do so.

Simplicity requires both renewed awareness and courageous action, which starts with slowing down. Adapting to our changing, complex world means being clear about our highest priorities, making room for what matters most, being able to expand our capacity to be aware of what is present in the moment, and then moving forward with this new awareness. This level of awareness and action is not reached by more manic busyness. We must not allow ourselves to confuse franticness with being adaptive.

Let the change in the world begin with me. Simplicity can be found within. The mind of the calm person is like the surface of a still pond. It reflects the beauty that surrounds it. Whereas the distressed mind, like the distressed surface of a pond, gives back a distorted reflection of its surroundings. Adhering to a practice that will invite simplicity will smooth the surface of the pond.

173

Reflect and then Act:

Build your knowledge of yourself, and your path to the future, by reflecting on your defining values. Begin by making a list of all the values that are important in your life. This will require some reflection. Once you have a list that feels complete, consider these values two at a time. Keep the most important of the pair, and for now discard the other. Continue working through your list—through the quarter-final and the semi-final elimination rounds if necessary—until you have narrowed the list down to five key values. Finally, place these values in order from the most to the least important. I know it is difficult to choose, but do it anyway—you can always change the order (or the list) later.

Align with your values. Draft a personal constitution, listing in order of priority your five or six most important governing values. Now, open up your calendar or day planner. Take a look at your activities for the past week and for the coming week. Ask yourself, to what degree do your daily activities reflect your defining values? Find a blank page, and create an imaginary schedule for a values-based day. What would your daily life look like if you lived from your defining values? How many changes do you need to make to get there? There's no need to make all these changes tomorrow, but pick one. Every step you take creates a new beginning.

Reflect on what you might be able to take out of your day—just for today—to make room for what matters most. Then try this again tomorrow. What habits would you like to make a part of your life that will carry you with stability down the river of life? Who can support you with this? Take one habit at a time, and practice it for a month until the new habits form a new way of life.

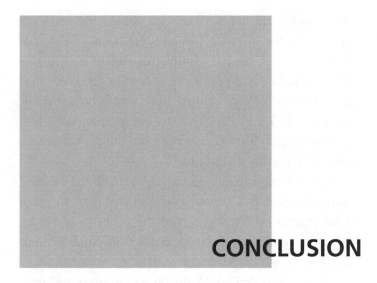

CONCLUSION

There once lived not far from the River Indus an ancient Persian by the name of Ali Hafed, who owned a very large farm of orchards, grain fields, and gardens. Indeed, Ali Hafed[1] was a wealthy and contented man.

One day a very old Buddhist priest visited the old Persian farmer. Together they sat down by the fire as the priest told him how this world of ours was made. He said that the world was once a bank of fog, and that the Almighty thrust his hand into this bank of fog, and began slowly moving his finger around, increasing the speed until at last he whirled this bank of fog into a solid ball of fire. Then it went rolling through the universe, burning its way through other banks of fog, and condensed the moisture without, until it fell in floods

---

[1] This story was inspired from the classic book, *Acres of Diamonds*, by Russell H Conwell, Jove Books, NYC, 1960.

of rain upon its hot surface and cooled the outward crust. Then the internal fires bursting outward through the crust threw up the mountains and hills, the valleys, the plains, and prairies of this wonderful world of ours. As this internal molten mass came bursting out and cooled, it very quickly became granite; then less quickly copper. With even more time the mass became gold, and, finally, diamonds.

The old priest then began to expound on the value of diamonds, that if a person had one diamond the size of his thumb he could purchase the country, and if he had a mine of diamonds he could place his children upon thrones through the influence of their great wealth.

When Ali Hafed heard all about diamonds and how much they were worth, he went to bed that night a poor man. He had not lost a thing, but he was suddenly poor because he was now discontented—because he feared he was poor. He said, "I want a mine of diamonds," and he lay fervently awake all night.

Resolved to be immensely rich, the farmer set out the next morning to find his fortune. He sold his farm, collected his money, left his family in the charge of a neighbor, and away he went in search of diamonds. He started at the Mountains of the Moon, came around into Palestine, then wandered into Europe, and at last, when all his money was spent, and he was in rags, wretched and poor, he stood on the shore in Barcelona, Spain, when a great tidal wave came rolling in. At that moment, the poor, afflicted, suffering, dying man could not resist the awful temptation to cast himself into that incoming tide, and he sank beneath its foaming crest, never to rise in this life again.

Back home, the man who had purchased Ali Hafed's farm was one day letting his camel drink from the garden brook. As the camel put its nose into the shallow water of that garden brook, Ali Hafed's successor noticed a curious flash of light from the white sands of the stream. He pulled out a black stone with an eye of light reflecting all the hues of the rainbow. And behold, below that black stone was discovered the diamond mine of Golcanda, the most magnificent diamond mine in all the history of mankind. Had Ali Hafed remained at home and dug in his own cellar, looked underneath his own wheat fields, or dug a hole in his own garden, he would have had "acres of diamonds" instead of wretchedness, starvation, and death by suicide in a strange land.

One can interpret this story in many ways and can glean many lessons, such as the corroding power of greed or the hell of unbridled desire. What struck me, when reading this story in the context of concluding a book about living life more simply, is that many of us dash around trying to uncover things that will have value in our lives, when the most important diamonds we can discover often lie within ourselves. Having read this far, you are a seeker of wisdom and that in itself will help you live life more simply. Stop and listen to the good judgment within you. I have hopefully

179

CONCLUSION

opened some doors to inspire and guide you to look within. If you make time to slow down and search inside yourself, you will find the diamonds that will help you make an art of living more simply.

In Erich Fromm's wonderful book, *The Art of Loving*,[2] he states that there are three steps we take to make an art of something. *First,* we must acquire knowledge; *second,* we must put our knowledge into practice; and *third,* we must have a burning desire to make this an art in our life. Making living simply an art requires you to keep your attention on the path. It means uncovering those magnificent human qualities and capabilities we all possess: awareness, patience, compassion, responsibility, honesty, courage, and perseverance. As we find and express these within ourselves, we can expand them to the world around us and realize these qualities are as precious to the survival of our planet and the well-being of its inhabitants as diamonds are to human wealth. And perhaps, on the journey, we will create a world a little less complex and a little more nourishing. Recognizing and appreciating the humanness in all humanity brings us to the heart of simple living.

I began this book with the notion that living simply is really about making room each day, to come home to yourself, and I leave you with a poem by David Whyte, entitled "The House of Belonging."[3]

[2] Erich Fromm, *The Art of Loving*, Harper and Row, New York: 1956.
[3] David Whyte, *The House of Belonging*, Many Rivers Press, Langley, Washington, 1999, pp. 4–6.

I awoke
this morning
in the gold light
turning this way
and that

thinking for
a moment
it was one
day
like any other.

But
the veil had gone
from my
darkened heart
and
I thought

it must have been the quiet
candlelight
that filled my room,

it must have been
the first
easy rhythm
with which I breathed
myself to sleep,

it must have been
the prayer I said
speaking to the otherness
of the night.

CONCLUSION

And
I thought
this is the good day
you could
meet your love,

this is the black day
someone close
to you could die.

This is the day
you realize
how easily the thread
is broken
between this world
and the next

and I found myself
sitting up
in the quiet pathway
of light,

the tawny
close grained cedar
burning round
me like fire
and all the angels of this housely
heaven ascending
through the first
roof of light
the sun has made.

This is the bright home
in which I live,
this is where
I ask
my friends
to come,
this is where I want
to love all the things
it has taken me so long
to learn to love.

This is the temple
of my adult aloneness
and I belong
to that aloneness
as I belong to my life.

There is no house
like the house of belonging.

May this book inspire and be a guide to you as you continue to find and polish your inner diamonds and find your house of belonging. For it is within this house you will discover simplicity.

It is said that soon after his enlightenment the Buddha was passed by a man on the road who was struck by the Buddha's extraordinary radiance and peaceful presence. The man stopped and asked the Buddha, "My friend, what are you? Are you a celestial being or a god?"

"No," said the Buddha.

"Well, then are you some kind of magician or wizard?" Again the Buddha answered, "No."

"Are you a man?"

"No."

"Well, my friend, then what are you?"

The Buddha replied, "I am awake."

I hope that, through these pages, you have been awakened.

When I come to the completion of a book, I always feel advanced in my own development. You the reader, and I, the author, create this work together, plowing the fields and planting the seeds for a future harvest. Hopefully, the words between these covers have been both livening and disturbing, for both are necessary for a renewed life. May we each continue the conversation we have started.

One Day at a Time—The Habits of Simplicity

"Your life will never change until you change something you do daily. The secret of simplicity is found in your daily routine."

— David Irvine

"It is not the mountain we conquer, it is ourselves," wrote Edmund Hillary, the famous Mount Everest adventurer. The mountain is us. If I want a simpler life, let it begin with me. If I change, the world will change. Breaking free of some of my old habits and attachments to overwork and busyness requires renewed clarity, courage, and a commitment to take small steps daily. Below is a suggested list of some actions you can begin today to start simplifying your life. It is not my intention to complicate your life with yet another "to-do" list. We are all unique and our needs change over time, so simply read over this list and pick one habit that fits for you today, and take a small action toward simplifying your life.

- Before you start your day make it a habit to ask yourself this one question: "What can I *take out* of my day today to make room for what matters most?"
- Get outdoors sometime during the day. Entrain to the rhythm of nature. The natural world will teach us about simplicity and, if you are open to it, you will find simplicity on the path.
- Spend time with children or elders. Listen to them. Learn from them. They have much to teach us about living life more simply.
- Make room—at least once a day—for some solitude and silence, to meditate, to pray, or to attend to the voice within.
- Start your day slowly. Take time to center yourself before meeting the world.
- Get a good night's sleep.
- Give yourself permission to cry once in awhile. A good cry is like a downpour after a drought. It's cleansing and healing.
- Take a nap.

- Don't watch the news before you go to bed. Most news is designed to entertain us—by entraining us to the dramas and the tragedies of the world. We all seem to have a love affair with the news, perhaps because it is a substitute for the real story, and the truth is too uncomfortable to face at times. Spend time winding down at the end of the day by being gentle with your soul. Find something that relaxes you at the end of the day. You'll sleep better.
- Pick *one* social cause to be committed to. Being of service to your family and community can bring per-spective and simplicity to your life, but spreading yourself too thin will erode it.
- Learn, at times, to let the phone ring without answer-ing it—at meal times, in conversation with important people, during your quiet times. If that is too big a leap, just turn the ringer off so you won't be tempt-ed to answer.
- Live in a house that costs you less than you can afford. If you are committed to simplicity, the practice of spending below your means in all areas of your life is an important habit.
- Turn off technology every so often. Shut down the computer. Turn off the cell phone. Unplug the televi-sion and the radio.
- Read poetry.
- Remember—everything in moderation. It is an old adage and a good reminder today.

Suggested Reading List: Where to Go If You Want More

Foster, Richard. *Freedom in Simplicity: Finding Harmony in a Complex World*. HarperCollins Publishers, 1981.
For those interested in understanding simplicity from a Christian perspective, you will find value in the timeless principles that Richard Foster outlines in this book.

Irvine, David. *Becoming Real: Journey to Authenticity*. DC Press, Sanford, Florida, 2003. (Phone: 866.602.1476)
To support you on your journey to simplicity, this book takes you further along the path of authentic living.

Izzo, John. *Second Innocence, Rediscovering Joy and Wonder* (A Guide to Renewal in Work, Relationships and Daily Life). Berrett-koehler, 2004.
John's skillful observations of the human condition, his spiritual insights and thoughtful and amusing anecdotes of his personal experiences guide the reader to the discovery of their own "second innocence"—the reawakening of their true self. This is a truly engaging and enlightening book for those who yearn for more meaning and peace in their lives.

Kabat-Zinn, Jon. *Wherever You Go There You Are: Mindfulness and Meditation in Everyday Life.* Hyperion, New York, 1994.
To live more simply, you must develop the art of paying attention, of listening to your heart. Rather than withdrawing from the world in order to find simplicity, Jon provides you with a good understanding of the tool of meditation, which will help you enjoy the world more fully, effectively, and peacefully.

Klatt, Bruce, Shaun Murphy, and David Irvine. *Accountability: Getting a Grip on Results.* Bow River Publishing, Calgary, 2003.
This book offers a practical philosophy for simplifying your work life and amplifying your impact through more focused conversations and intentional commitments.

Lazear, Jonathon. *Meditations for Men Who Do Too Much.* Simon & Schuster, New York, A Fireside/Parkside Meditation Book, 1992.
This very helpful book, with a reading for each day of the year, is useful for men who want to break free of the vicious daily cycle of work, achievement, and acquisition. There is also a companion book for women: Schaef, Ann Wilson, *Meditations for Women Who Do Too Much*, HarperCollins, San Francisco, 1997. Both Jonathon and Anne have impacted my life deeply.

Lazear, Jonathon. *The Man Who Mistook His Job for a Life*. Crown Publishers, New York, 2001.
This is Jonathon's personal story of his recovery from workaholism. Beyond telling his story, Jonathon also spells out both the cause and the cure.

Oliva, Max, S. J. *Free to Pray, Free to Love: Growing in Prayer and Compassion*. Ave Maria Press, Notre Dame, Indiana, 1999.
Max Oliva, a Jesuit Priest and personal friend, gives wonderful, practical guidance in his books for Christians who desire to live a more compassionate and contemplative life.

Palmer, Parker. *Let Your Life Speak: Listening to The Voice of Vocation*. Jossey-Bass, San Francisco, 2000.
Parker has had enormous impact on my work and my life, and this short book, full of wisdom, compassion, and humanity, will take you along the path to simple living and beyond.

Rechtschaffen, Stephan. *Time Shifting: Creating More Time to Enjoy Your Life*. Doubleday, New York, 1996.
This book will change your perception of time, not as a unit to be "managed," but as a quality of life. Stephan shows people a way to take each day as an opportunity for finding and expressing what matters most to you.

Rohn, Jim. *Cultivating Unshakeable Character,
Nightingale Conant Audio Cassette Series*. Niles,
Illinois, 1996. (Phone: 1.800.323.5552)
I have been deeply influenced by the words of Jim Rohn,
particularly in the area of building strong character. Even
though this cassette series doesn't relate specifically to
creating a simple life, it addresses the unseen roots of balanced living—strong character. Any of his audio CD's or
cassettes is worth listening to.

Segal, Jerome M. *Graceful Simplicity: Toward a
Philosophy and Politics of Simple Living*. Henry Holt &
Company, New York, 1999.
Segal offers a new vision for society that has application
at both a personal and political level. This is a very
thoughtful and provoking read that speaks about simplicity with a renewed and practical philosophy.

Simmons, Philip. *Learning to Fall: The Blessings of an
Imperfect Life*. Bantam Books, New York, 2000.
For those who wish to be inspired with a renewed perspective on life, this book is a blessing. This is Philip's
story of some of his final years of living with ALS, Lou
Gehrig's disease. Phil died shortly after this book was
published, but his legacy lives on in this extraordinary
piece of work.